PLACES OF THE IMAGINATION

T0361973

For Silvijn

Places of the Imagination
Media, Tourism, Culture

STIJN REIJNDERS
Erasmus University Rotterdam, the Netherlands

LONDON AND NEW YORK

First published 2011 by Ashgate Publishing

2 Park Square, Milton Park, Abingdon, Oxfordshire OX14 4RN
52 Vanderbilt Avenue, New York, NY 10017

Routledge is an imprint of the Taylor & Francis Group, an informa business

First issued in paperback 2020

British Library Cataloguing in Publication Data
Reijnders, Stijn, 1976-
　Places of the imagination : media, tourism, culture.
　1. Culture and tourism. 2. Motion picture locations--Case
　studies. 3. Television program locations--Case studies.
　4. Literary landmarks--Case studies.
　I. Title
　306.4'819-dc22

Library of Congress Cataloging-in-Publication Data
Reijnders, Stijn, 1976-
　Places of the imagination : media, tourism, culture / by Stijn Reijnders.
　　p. cm.
　Includes bibliographical references (p. 145) and index.
　ISBN 978-1-4094-1977-8 (hbk)
　1. Tourism--Social aspects. 2. Culture and tourism. I. Title.
　G155.A1R455 2011
　306.4'819--dc22

2011009737

ISBN 978-1-4094-1977-8 (hbk)
ISBN 978-0-367-60226-0 (pbk)

Contents

List of Figures

Foreword

For a long time the 'place' of media was forgotten. Writers even argued that media erased space, collapsed our sense of place. Yet all the time media was being made in particular places, sometimes places in full public view, but generally places which it was hard to access without the right industry-recognised credentials. And from the beginning of modern media, the physical trajectories of people or things *in* the media (celebrities, their clothes, possessions, sites of appearance) were followed closely. The crowds lining the streets of Manhattan in August 1926 for Rudolf Valentino's funeral are only one obvious early example.

It was a while however before the role of media production sites in everyday imagination became better noticed, first, as an object of tourism and second, as a topic of academic analysis. The first involved particularly the rise of tourism to sites of filming, television production and general media coverage, as part of the wider growth in leisure visits to sites of what Dean MacCannell called 'staged authenticity': media tourism gives 'authentic access' to the sites where media (fictional or factual) 'really does' get produced. Second, from the mid to late 1990s came the broadening of conventional agendas of media studies as a subject beyond texts, production and audiences, to include the wider processes (such as tourism and ritual) related to, and formed around, the media process.

I became interested in media tourism in the mid-1990s through this second route, rather than through a particular passion for media tourism, only to realise that I had always rather liked celebrity spotting, and 'being there' at the physical places where moments in media narratives were enacted. In fact, the convergence of an interest in media tourism and wider questions of media power had shaped my attention to media ever since I stood fascinated in a field in Oxford in 1994 as then US President Bill Clinton's helicopter landed for a visit to his university *alma mater*. That fascination led to my concern with the intersections of media and place in *my* first book *The Place of Media Power*.

Media tourism remains in my view an extremely rich topic for research, whether anthropological, sociological or more closely textual and historical. Yet until now it has awaited a writer who can draw together its various strands and expound its key themes and features. That writer has now emerged in the person of the young Dutch scholar Stijn Reijnders.

I have followed with pleasure how Stijn's work has extended and enriched previous ideas on media tourism, including my own, towards a broader model for grasping the *variety* of media tourism and its dynamics. This book is a fascinating and vivid summation of his work on media tourism so far and, in my view, makes a decisive contribution towards finally grasping media tourism, and the practices of imagination condensed within it, as the rich, if neglected, sites for hermeneutic and historical inquiry that throughout modernity they have been.

Nick Couldry
Goldsmiths, University of London

Acknowledgements

This book, and the original research project, was made possible by a three-year research grant for innovational research from the Netherlands Organisation for Scientific Research (NWO). I would further like to thank the many colleagues and friends who have contributed to the development and refinement of this project with their valuable comments: especially Liesbet van Zoonen, Gerard Rooijakkers, José van Dijck, Joke Hermes, Linda Duits, Vincent Crone, Jeroen de Kloet, Giselinde Kuipers, but also Martin Millband, Pep Dros, Bas van Druiten, Ties Knapen, and last but not least, Elvire Jansen. Many thanks to Nick Couldry, for writing the Foreword to this book.

The results of the research have previously been published in various academic periodicals. First, parts of the section on television detectives have been published in the *European Journal of Communication* (Reijnders 2009b) and *Cultural Geographies* (Reijnders 2010d), and the Dutch journals *Tijdschrift voor Mediageschiedenis* (Reijnders 2009a) and *Tijdschrift voor Communicatiewetenschap* (Reijnders 2009c). Second, findings from the research into James Bond have previously been published in *Area* (Reijnders 2010a) and *Sociologie* (Reijnders 2010c). Lastly, parts of the Dracula chapters have previously been published in *Annals of Tourism Research* (Reijnders 2011) and the Dutch *Toerisme Studies* (Reijnders 2010b). My thanks to these journals for their valuable reviews and for their permission for partial reuse of existing fragments of text.

When an individual enters an imaginary realm, he typically finds himself in a place where he is not alone.

John Caughey (1984: 28–9)

Chapter 1
Introduction

On a pleasant summer's day, a visitor to Exeter College, one of the oldest colleges in Oxford, has a good chance of coming across a group of tourists. Of course, there is nothing unusual in this: most colleges attract a constant stream of tourists. But these visitors are not looking at the lovely, neo-Gothic chapel or the view of Radcliffe Square. Instead, they are pointing their cameras at a corner of the lawn, an apparently insignificant bit of grass. It is also striking that the normal chatter of tourists has given way to a solemn silence, where the only sound to be heard is the clicking of camera shutters. What's happening here? This is the exact place where Inspector Morse – the main character in the television series of the same name – was struck down by a heart attack. In the last episode of the detective series, which was popular around the world, Inspector Morse collapsed, at just this spot on the lawn of Exeter College, to pass away several hours later in a local hospital.

Figure 1.1   Tourists take photographs of the lawn at Exeter College during the Inspector Morse Tour

Source: Photograph by Elvire Jansen.

In Search of Morse

For more than ten years, the Inspector Morse Tour has been one of the most popular tours in Oxford. Despite the fact that the series ended in 2000, every year a steady stream of around 3,500 tourists still pay to follow in the footsteps of the rather sombre, melancholic Inspector Morse and his assistant, Lewis.[1] Taking approximately two hours, the tour takes the tourists past the most important film locations in the centre of Oxford, from fictional crime scenes to Morse and Lewis' favourite pubs. The link to Morse is visibly honoured in some of these locations. Thus, the Randolph Hotel has a special 'Morse Bar', whose walls are covered with photographs of the actors in the company of Colin Dexter, the author of the Morse series.

The Inspector Morse Tour is no isolated incident. In other cities similar tours are organized at the locations of popular films, television series or novels. For example, New York has its Sex and the City Tour, in which buses full of *Sex and the City* fans motor through the city, past the apartments, cafes and clothes shops that are featured in the series. In the same way, fans of *Dracula* get their kicks in the Romanian province of Transylvania.

One of the most large-scale examples of recent years is perhaps *The Lord of the Rings*, which has inspired thousands upon thousands of 'jet-setters' to set off for New Zealand. Although precise figures are unavailable, there are estimates of noticeable increases in the number of tourists from overseas in the first few years after the release of this globally popular film trilogy. These fans received a warm welcome in New Zealand and continue to do so. In some cases almost literally: anyone arriving at Wellington airport at that time was made officially welcome to 'Middle Earth'. Numerous local businesses and travel agencies capitalized on this new trend and it is rumoured that the New Zealanders themselves were actually proud of the increase in interest in their country (Beeton 2005; Roesch 2009).

Nevertheless, this form of tourism is not always welcomed everywhere with open arms. A notorious example of this is the novel *The Da Vinci Code* and the eponymous film, which, at the beginning of the last decade, prompted a genuine boom in the number of visitors to locations in Paris, London and Rosslyn. The Louvre Museum in Paris attracted a record number of visitors in 2005. It turned out that this interest was not generated by a particular exhibition but by the fact that this temple of the fine arts had figured in the popular thriller *The Da Vinci Code*. Thousands of people made their way to the Louvre in order to see with their own eyes the spot where the fictional murder in the thriller had taken place (Braun 2006). A similar fate befell the little Rosslyn Chapel, which became one of the most popular tourist destinations in Scotland as a result of *The Da Vinci Code*, complete with crush barriers, entrance gates and a gift shop next door. The director of the Rosslyn Chapel resigned during the course of 2006. He could no longer bear the sight of this, for him, holy place being turned into 'The Da Vinci Code Disneyland' (Johnston 2006).

---

1 Figures based on personal correspondence with the Oxford Tourist Information Centre.

Figure 1.2   Travellers to Wellington Airport were welcomed to 'Middle-earth'

Note: The première of *The Lord of the Rings* stimulated an enormous amount of tourism to New Zealand. Thousands upon thousands of fans went off in search of the locations of this world famous film trilogy.
Source: Photograph by Stijn Reijnders.

Media tourism

Strictly speaking, the fact that tourists are drawn to the scene of a fictional story is not a new phenomenon. An early example of this would be the British detective Sherlock Holmes, whose supposed home 221b Baker Street already attracted visitors at the beginning of the twentieth century (Wheeler 2003). In a more general sense, these tourists are part of a longer tradition of literary tourism. In her book *The Literary Tourist* (2006), the British literary scholar Nicola Watson describes how a fascination developed in the nineteenth century for the graves of famous authors, the houses where they were born, as well as the settings they described in their works, such as Sir Walter Scott's Loch Katrine or the Brontë sisters' Haworth (cf. Seaton 1998; Hardyment 2000). In the oral folk tradition, there is an even longer tradition of 'legend trips', where people traveled to locations – castles, bridges or cemeteries – associated with popular ghost stories (Ellis 1989, 2001).

**Figure 1.3   Sir Arthur Conan Doyle set the house of fictitious detective
Sherlock Holmes at 221b Baker Street**

Note: In 1990 the Sherlock Holmes Museum was set up at this location. The layout of the
museum is based on descriptions from the books.
Source: Photograph by Stijn Reijnders.

Nevertheless, there would seem to be an increase in scale and a popularization
of such trips in the current age. In the nineteenth century, literary tourism was
limited, with some notable exceptions, to a relative small group of lovers of
literature (Watson 2006: 131–200), whereas each of the contemporary TV tours
attracts thousands of tourists every year. Visiting 'fictional' locations from
'low culture' has grown into an important economic activity, with far-reaching
consequences for the communities involved, the local inhabitants, and the tourists
themselves (Beeton 2005). These tours provide the framework within which
many people get to know a new city such as Oxford, New York or Ystad. This
can no longer be considered a rare activity, but rather a widespread phenomenon:
a growing niche in the global tourist market, variously labelled 'TV tourism',
'movie tourism', 'movie-induced tourism' or 'film-induced tourism' (Beeton
2005).[2] In this book I have chosen to introduce a more inclusive term: 'media

---

2   Although figures relating to the worldwide impact of TV and film on tourist
behaviour are scarce, there is ample anecdotal evidence that, from the 1980s onwards, more

tourism'. Not only does this term do justice to the rich history of literary tourism, it also recognizes the multimedia character of many contemporary examples such as *Inspector Morse*, *Lord of the Rings* and *The Da Vinci Code*.

Little is known about the popularity of these TV detective tours. Influenced by post-modern philosophies about hyper-reality (Baudrillard 1981) and de-territorialization (Deleuze and Guattari 1988), communication scholars have, for a long time, predominantly emphasized the virtual character of our media culture. Following the work of Baudrillard, the general argument goes that post-modern individuals can no longer distinguish between what is real and what is not because of the excess of media images to which they are exposed. Even more, the virtual media world has become their most important frame of reference. According to this argument, people would no longer need to travel, since they could experience 'virtual tourism' just by watching television (Gibson 2006). Based on these prevailing theoretical models, it is difficult to explain why people make the effort to travel to a place with which they are already familiar from the media (Rojek 1993a: 69–72).

Recently, partly in response to these post-modern philosophies, interest in the material, more physical aspects of our media culture has grown – a development that within media studies has been called the 'spatial turn' (Falkheimer and Jansson 2006). Because of this, the phenomenon of media tourism has also come more under the spotlight.

For example, studies have described the attraction of the set of *Coronation Street* at Granada Studios near Manchester (Couldry 2000) and the Manhattan TV Tour in New York (Torchin 2002). Other scholars have focused on the popularity of *Blade Runner* in Los Angeles (Brooker 2005), *Braveheart* in Scotland (Edensor 2005), *The Sound of Music* in Salzburg (Roesch 2009), the *X-Files*, *Smallville* and *Battlestar Galactica* in Vancouver (Brooker 2007), *Harry Potter* settings in the UK (Iwashita 2006), and sites where *The Lord of the Rings* was shot in New Zealand (Tzanelli 2004, 2007; Beeton 2005; Roesch 2009). In addition, studies have described the effects of these tours on the local community. For example, Mordue (2001) interviewed residents of Goathland, after the village became a tourist hotspot as a result of the British TV series *Heartbeat*. Similarly, Beeton (2005: 123–9) looked at the effects of tourism in Barwond Heads, the Australian village that served as the backdrop for the popular movie, *Sea Change*.

This signifies the emergence of a recognized, interdisciplinary field of research, consisting of aspects of, among other things, media studies, communication science, tourism studies, cultural geography and fan studies. In spite of the increasing interest in the phenomenon of media tourism, many questions remain as yet unanswered. Little is known about the dimension of media tourism relating to content: why do some media products lead to media tourism while others don't? What characteristics of a story contribute to its attraction? Do different genres

---

and more tourists visit the locations from their favourite TV serial or movie (Beeton 2005: 20–40).

**Figure 1.4   Participants in the Sex and the City Tour enjoying a
Cosmopolitan in the bar from the television series**

Source: Photograph by Maria Heemskerk.

possibly lead to various sub-forms of media tourism? These questions have in part, already been posed in existing studies (cf. Roesch 2009), but no satisfactory answer has as yet been forthcoming.

An underlying, more philosophical question concerns the relationship between the story and its represented landscape. Are the origins of media tourism entirely contained in the story, which ascribes meaning to the represented landscape? Or should the answer be sought in the landscape itself, which as a physical-material actuality plays an active role in the creation of certain stories? Many stories do indeed seem to be anchored in a particular landscape. By way of illustration: *Dracula* finds a logical home in the mysterious mist-encircled mountainous landscape of Transylvania. It is difficult to imagine that Stoker would have chosen to set his story of the bloodthirsty count in, for example, a Dutch Polder. Has the popularity of the Dracula tours, then, entirely arisen out of the story, does it lie in the landscape or is it a combination of the two? And if it is a combination, how does such an assemblage come about?

Besides this, what are the consequences of media tourism for the local communities? Media tourism often follows a capricious pattern: it emerges suddenly but can just as quickly vanish again when the public becomes gripped by some new blockbuster. What consequences do these unpredictable tourist streams have for those who – not necessarily through their own design – have to deal with them? The commercial, socio-political and ecological consequences vary widely in each case, but it may also be possible to discern more widespread patterns.

Finally, one of the most important questions, about which we are still groping in the dark, is the meaning that media tourism has for the tourists themselves. It is remarkable that we know so little about this, for it is precisely the personal experiences of the fan/tourist and the meaning that they ascribe to the event that form the crux of the entire phenomenon. There, in the head and heart of the fan/tourist, resides the fascination and motivation to visit these locations. That is where the initial moment of connection takes place, the moment in which the world of the imagination temporarily comes together with – or perhaps perfectly contrasts with – the sensory experience of physical reality. The essence thus lies in penetrating more deeply the world of the imagination. A quest of this sort, however, demands a theoretical perspective, which, like a compass, can give direction to our research.

Figure 1.5   Various travel guides specialized in media tourism

Note: These travel guides provide information about the locations where well-known films and television series were shot.

Source: Photograph by Stijn Reijnders.

Places of the Imagination

With that aim in mind, the following chapter will introduce a new approach. The point of departure is the research of French historian Pierre Nora into the working of collective memory. In the 1980s, Nora showed how *lieux de mémoire* such as national monuments and battlefields act as a validation of collective memory. In the same way, as will be more comprehensively illustrated in the following chapter, we can also speak of *lieux d'imagination* (places of the imagination) which are not so much concerned with collective memory, as collective imagination. *Lieux d'imagination* are physical locations, which serve as a symbolic anchor for the collective imagination of a society. By visiting these locations, tourists are able to construct and 'validate' a symbolic distinction between imagination and reality.

In the following chapters, the concept of *lieux d'imagination* (places of the imagination) shall be applied to, and at the same refined by, three actual examples of media tourism. The first part of this research shall involve an international comparison of three popular TV detectives, who each have inspired significant tourist streams: *Inspector Morse* in Oxford, *Baantjer* in Amsterdam and *Wallander* in the Swedish coastal town of Ystad. The comparison starts with a textual analysis of the content of these series: I shall investigate what role or meaning representations of local landscapes (or cityscapes) have within the narrative structure and development of *Inspector Morse*, *Baantjer* and *Wallander*. I shall also pay attention to the relationship between the subject matter of the content and its exploitation for tourism purposes. For example, it is remarkable that a sleepy provincial town such as Ystad – where in actuality, there are hardly any murders – can reinvent itself as 'Wallander's Ystad' and thereby appeal to the popularity of a series, in which the most gruesome murders follow each other in quick succession. What do these stories have to do with the hitherto innocent landscape of Ystad? After that, the comparison will be extended to the situation in the locations themselves: how did media tourism begin and what developments have these places of the imagination seen through time? Which social actors have played a decisive role?

The second part of this research shall focus on one of the most long-lasting and successful film series of all time: James Bond. Over a period of almost 50 years, 23 'official' James Bond films have been released. In his attempts to save the Western World from the forces of Evil, 007 has encountered a wide range of countries, exotic islands and 'thrilling' international cities. Although a number of these locations have grown into tourist hotspots – note, for example, the popularity of 'James Bond Island' – most of these locations attract only a limited number of tourists. James Bond tourism is first and foremost an individual affair, in which people who have been fans for years (mostly white, middle-aged men) try to follow the trail of 007 and to document it, so that they can have some localized memento of their hero. It is these so-called 'media pilgrimages' to the world of Bond, that will be central to the second part of this research. I shall investigate how these trips are organized, what ritual meaning they have and what significance being on the spot has for Bond fans.

The third and last section of this research is dedicated to one of the greatest anti-heroes in popular culture: Count Dracula. Every year thousands of tourists flock to Transylvania, on the trail of Count Dracula. They are inspired by Bram Stoker's novel *Dracula* or one of the many film versions of the twentieth or twenty-first centuries. I shall look into what exactly drives these people and what significance they derive from their trip. The emphasis in this part, therefore, will lie explicitly on how the tourists experience their trip. In order to be able to investigate this world, research was conducted during the Dracula Tour – a seven-day bus journey through Transylvania – and through participation in a literary walking tour through Whitby, a coastal town in North-east England.

Each section of the research shall consider the same dimensions: attention will be paid to the content of the media products concerned, to the way in which the local community has anticipated the media product and to the tourists' perception of their experiences. At the same time, mutual differences in content and local practice make it possible to lay a slightly different accent on each section of the research. It is precisely these small shifts in emphasis that can enrich the analysis and bring about synergy between the separate areas of research.

In the closing chapter, the individual analyses shall be compared with each other, in an attempt to present an integrated picture of media tourism as a cultural phenomenon. What conclusions can be drawn on the basis of the fieldwork in Oxford, Amsterdam, Ystad, Jamaica, London, Whitby and Transylvania? What lessons are to be learned from this journey through the twilight between imagination and imagined?

THEORETICAL FRAMEWORK

Chapter 2
Places of the Imagination

In this chapter, the foundations for a new theoretical perspective on media tourism shall be established. This perspective will be based on a combination of the work of the French historian Pierre Nora and the American anthropologist John Caughey. Central to this theme will be the introduction of a new concept: *lieux d'imagination*.

In Memoria

In the mid-1980s, Pierre Nora introduced the concept *lieux de mémoire*. According to Nora, modern, Western society was characterized by an obsession with the past. With the loosening of traditional social bonds, individuals and social groups were desperately in search of the roots of a shared identity. This had brought about a rich culture of memorialization, in Nora's interpretation. *Lieux de mémoire* had an important role in this, as places which can function as symbolic moorings in a turbulent world. These were generally physical places, such as memorials, monuments, or specific locations. In this way, Nora applied the term to the battlefields of Verdun, which had acquired an important, almost mythical status after the First World War, as a place to remember and memorialize the war. In addition, Nora applied the term *lieux de mémoire* to metaphorical places, like certain songs or celebrations (Nora 1984–1992).

Nora's ideas about the modern culture of memorialization have provided the foundation for a thorough and currently well-known series of studies of *lieux de mémoire* in France. Beside this, his work has been followed in other countries, among them Germany (Francois and Schulze 2001) and the Netherlands (De Boer and Frijhoff 1993; Wesseling 2005). What makes his approach so appealing is, in the first place, that he emphasized the constructed nature of memory. By showing how social institutions both consciously and subconsciously influence the way a society recollects its past and gives form to it, Nora broke with the neo-Durkheiman tradition, which interprets collective memory as an organic system (Legg 2005). He thus joined a new movement in the field of historic sciences, which among other things found expression in the study of 'invented traditions' (Hobsbawm and Ranger 1983). Secondly, Nora had a sharp eye for humankind's 'topophilic' nature. He pointed out the general need to identify certain places as holy, and to use these places as physical points of reference for a phenomenon whose essence is non-physical. Apparently people need physical objects and places to give form to their memory, Nora proposed, as a way of 'congealing' time (cf. Bruno 2003).

Nora is usually considered a deconstructivist, since he did not investigate the historical event *an sich*, but the way in which the memory of this historical event took shape later. Though he did also consider non-physical locations, the emphasis for him lay in concrete, determinable places, where certain historical events had taken place in the past. In this sense, Nora did not take deconstructionism to its logical extreme; the historical authenticity of an actual location remained the point of departure.

The question remains whether the historical authenticity of a certain location is a necessary ingredient for the processes that Nora was investigating. Locations can serve equally well as the setting for a memorialization of something that never took place. This is certainly the case, for example, with instances of media tourism, which are mainly based on memorializing and reliving a *fictional* event. As a result it would appear justified, in cases such as these, to take the process of memorializing itself, and the resultant need for locations, as our starting point, rather than the actual historical location. Using this inverted logic, every possible location could, in principle, be suitable to memorialize and commodify an event, whether actual or fictional. Of course, in practice certain locations will definitely be more 'authentic' than others, though in this sense of the word, authenticity is something subjectively assigned to the place by individuals or groups, among them, for example, historians. The historical record definitely no longer has the monopoly on authentic place; geographical realism in fiction can also grant authenticity to a certain location.

In an attempt to make this alternative approach more concrete, in this chapter I shall introduce a new concept. *Lieux d'imagination* ('places of the imagination') are material reference points like objects or places, which for certain groups within society serve as material-symbolic references to a common imaginary world.[1] Imagination for this purpose can be defined as a mental conception of an object, person or event that at a certain time and in a certain place is not actually present. Memory in this context is nothing more, or less, than the imagination of an event from the past. Imagination can make reference to the past, but not necessarily so. It is also possible to imagine an event taking place elsewhere but in the same time period. Imagination of future events is also not beyond the realm of possibility. How many locations have been imagined before they became reality? Or as Edmundo O'Gorman put it: 'America was invented before it was discovered' (O'Gorman 1961). By shifting the emphasis from memory to imagination, the constructed and interrelated character of both phenomena can be further examined.

---

1   For sake of clarity, the English term 'places of the imagination' will be used in the remaining part of this book.

Appearance and Reality

This conceptual adjustment does raise some questions. First, there is the important question of a phenomenological explanation. Why do people need physical points of reference for their imagination? Nora maintained that this need is the result of an obsession with the past. But this does not always appear to be the case, for the simple reason that the concept 'places of the imagination' does not *per se* refer to the past. An alternative explanation can be found in the work of the cultural anthropologist John Caughey.

According to Caughey (1984), people live in two distinct worlds. On the one hand, they find themselves in the 'real' world, an empirically measurable reality, defined by time and place. On the other hand, there is a world of imagination, an interconnected complex of fantasies, daydreams and stories. Though these worlds are usually separated from each other, says Caughey, there are moments when both coincide temporarily. Such moments are meaningful, because they bring two elements together: the quotidian becomes unusual, while at the same time the strange and unknown is made usual (Caughey 1984).

Caughey's theory fits in a long, though admittedly rather subordinate, tradition in philosophy, which emphasizes the importance of *place* in the development of imagination. As Jeff Malpas argues in *Place and Experience* (1999), people's imagination is inextricably connected to their concrete, sensory experience of place. Even the wildest fantasies spring from something recognizable, for the simple reason that there would be no way to picture them otherwise. And not only do thoughts, fantasies and concepts spring from physical experiences, but, according to Malpas, they constantly seek confirmation from those physical experiences, mirroring it (Malpas 1999). The converse is also true. As the philosopher Immanuel Kant hypothesized two centuries earlier, it is impossible to conceive of a coherent picture of 'the' actuality or 'the' reality, without in some way making use of your imagination (Huppauf and Wolf 2009: 2).

One of the problems with Caughey's theory, though, is that it's based on a binary opposition between an 'imagined' and a 'real' world. This imagination/reality dichotomy has been problematized in recent film theory (Creswell and Dixon 2002; Lukinbeal 2004; Aitken and Dixon 2006; Hanna 2000). As stated by Stuart Aitken and Deborah Dixon: 'we can no longer talk of film representing, or mimicking, reality, because we can no longer assume that there is a single, coherent reality waiting out there to be filmed' (Aitken and Dixon 2006: 326). In addition, media scholars have shown how different TV and film genres create their own 'reality-effect' (Black 2002; Clark and Doel 2005). In other words, it seems more justified to talk about a complex of multiple imaginations and realities, than about two separate worlds.

However, this problem can be easily overcome by re-interpreting Caughey's 'world of imagination' and 'real world' as two *emic* concepts, as part of how people try to categorize their own everyday life. Because imaginations and realities are interwoven, people feel the need to unravel them. Thus, places of the imagination should not be interpreted as physical points of reference to an existing, factual opposition between 'imagination' and 'reality', but as locations where the symbolic difference between these two concepts is being (re-)constructed by those involved, based on what is considered 'factual' evidence.

A second question about the concept 'places of the imagination' is its historical uniqueness. Nora puts his analysis explicitly in the context of Modernism, a period which he sees as characterized by the erosion of traditional social bonds and the resultant desire for a shared past. This leads to the question to what extent the concept 'places of the imagination' is also explicitly associated with Modernism. Just a glance into history seems sufficient to discount this question. Far before the Modern era, great journeys were undertaken to visit places associated with the world of the imagination. As described in the introduction, there is a longstanding tradition of literary tourism and legend tripping, but at the same time, one cannot deny the strong increase in scale and the popularization of such trips in the current age.

The concept 'places of the imagination' is thus not new, but it has a new face today, being inextricably associated with the current media culture. We live in an age where the world of the imagination is primarily a media world, where television and the cinema have developed into the main storytellers of the age. If one looks for the material signs of this world of imagination, one quickly arrives at the film sets and locations used in the production of popular films and TV series.

In this regard, is there some connection with Jean Baudrillard's notion of 'hyperreality'? As set out in his introduction, Baudrillard posits the thesis that (post) modern man finds himself in an artificial world of artistic simulation, in which reproductions of reality have replaced every notion of reality. To what extent does this notion of hyperreality relate to the concept of 'places of the imagination'? Both concepts share the idea that reality and the imagination are somehow interwoven. In both approaches a great deal of attention is paid to the spatial dimension – Baudrillard's analysis focuses at length on the architecture and spatial arrangement of places like Las Vegas and Disneyworld.

That said, the concept of 'places of the imagination' differs in two crucial respects. First of all, Baudrillard presumes – as does Nora – a historical singularity. He suggests that hyperreality is a typically contemporary phenomenon that arises out of postmodern society. In the approach presented in this book, I point to the historical continuity between nineteenth- and eighteenth-century forms of media tourism and present-day examples. Underlying this is the supposition that for a long time a sort of zone of tension has existed between imagination and reality, but that at this point in time, this zone has possibly come more to the fore.

After this, Baudrillard's rhetoric veers off in the opposite direction – an inflation of hyperreality, through which contact with reality becomes completely lost. The approach set out in this book adopts a less pretentious position, by suggesting that there is a continuous and separate relationship between both concepts, through which neither is considered inferior, precisely because they both exist by the grace of the other.

Model

To resume, it is the proposition of this book that the phenomenon of media tourism derives its power and popularity from the symbolic contrast between imagination and reality. Imagination and reality are not interpreted as two static entities, but as cultural constructs, which have a relationship with each other that exemplifies the separation between them. This relationship can be interpreted as a circular process, through which experiencing a place (through the senses or through symbols) fulfills a key function. Seen from this process-driven perspective, it becomes clear that the concept of 'places of the imagination' not only involves the physical locations themselves but also the underlying process. It relates to how the imagination literally 'takes place'.

Figure 2.1 provides a schematic rendering of this process. It shows how artists – authors, scriptwriters, film directors – are inspired by their knowledge and experience of existing physical places (phase 1). After that they construct, using their creative imagination, stories that are played out in a specific time and place. Creative transformation is at the core of this process: artists transform existing texts, ideas, memories, sensory experiences and thoughts into a cultural

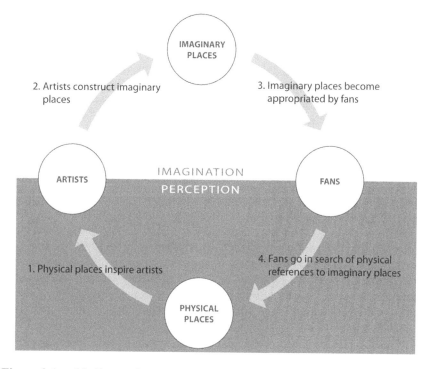

Figure 2.1   Media tourism as part of a circular process
Source: Model – Stijn Reijnders; Design – Ties Knapen.

product – a film, television series or book – with its own narrative space
(phase 2).

These imagined places become in their turn appropriated by fans or enthusiasts
– be they readers, the television audience or visitors to the cinema (phase 3).
Naturally, the images from a specific story, triggered in one's imagination do not
have to match those originally conceived by the artist. The 'coding' and 'decoding'
of a cultural product is a complex process, in which surface-noise, distortion and
creative appropriation are more the rule than the exception (Hall 2000). In this
sense, the cultural product provides the building blocks, with which the reader or
viewer can design for themselves an image of the story being told and of the space
in which the story is being played out. From this, a difference can also be found
between written and audiovisual cultural products, which each in different ways,
catch and stimulate the imagination.

Some of these fans subsequently decide to set off on the trail of physical
references to this imaginary world, which they themselves have appropriated
(phase 4). Where artists create an imaginary world on the basis of their experience
of physical places, for fans the process is reversed: they use the imagination as a
starting point and subsequently go and try to find in reality, material references
to the world of their imagination. Of course the stories offer some guidance
for these adventures. Many films, novels and television series make explicit
reference to existing places or regions, mostly with the intention of lending a
certain credibility to the product of the artist's imagination. However, as a rule,
these references confine themselves to establishing the story generally in a certain
city or region. It remains in most cases for the readers or viewers to fill in the
geographical blanks. That is also precisely what makes identifying localities such
an addictive activity: the fan is stimulated into giving meaning to what can only
be read between the lines.

It is not only fans who are involved in ascribing locations in 'reality' to
imagined places, but also local businesses and organizations. A striking example
of this is the Morse pubs in Oxford. Various bars in Oxford present themselves
as 'the' pub from Inspector Morse. They hang photographs of the filming on
their walls, have posters and paintings of Morse and – in one particular case –
even change the name of their establishment to capitalize on their association
with Morse. This is about more than just a brand name. By giving themselves
a place in the story, or, to put it better, by appropriating the story to their own
environment, these pubs lend Morse a certain authenticity. Morse has become
more and more regarded by many tourists as 'typically Oxford'. So now, by
profiling themselves as 'the' Morse pub, these bars succeed in acquiring not only
a reputation for themselves, but also a central position in 'the place myth' that
is called Oxford.

The example of Morse, in particular, is played out at a local level. However,
organizations are also involved in the localization of popular stories at a
regional and even at a national level. For example, the tourism office of the
British county of Kent recently arranged to have the region style itself as

'Bond County' because of its associations with James Bond and 007 author Ian Fleming.[2] Another example is the enthusiasm with which New Zealand's office of tourism leapt onto the *Lord of the Rings* bandwagon. Localization and the appropriation of popular stories from the media have become big business.

Similar commercial practices can also lead to a process that could be described as the 'sanctification' of a location. Dean McCannell in his now classic study *The Tourist: A New Theory of the Leisure Class* (1976) describes how places can be transformed into tourist attractions in five phases:

1. *Naming*;
2. *Framing and elevation*;
3. *Enshrinement*;
4. *Mechanical reproduction*; and
5. *Social reproduction.*

If applied to the phenomenon of media tourism, there could well be question marks placed beside McCannell's specific order of phases. The question arises of whether the phase called 'social reproduction' (the distribution of publicity about the location) should be the first rather than the last phase in the case of media tourism. Nevertheless, the concept of sanctification in a more general sense, still serves our purpose. I shall return to this theme in a later chapter.

To sum up, a new concept has been introduced in this chapter, elaborating on the existing concepts of *lieux de mémoire* and 'hyperreality'. While Nora's work indicates how authentic locations can stimulate the historical imagination, in this chapter the reverse process is described: how people actively go in search of material references to (re)confirm their notions of imagination and reality. *Lieux d'imagination* (places of the imagination) are defined as places of the imagination: material reference points which have a connection with certain stories. These places offer the opportunity, I would suggest, to construct a symbolic distinction between 'imagination' and 'reality'. Places of the imagination enjoy a long tradition, which stretches back to before the advent of mass media, but they do currently form an intrinsic portion of our media culture.

The starting point was that imagination and reality have an inherent bond with each other. Imagination emanates from sensory experience – making a creative adaptation of what is known – and conversely the power of the imagination is necessary to assemble all the sensory stimulants into a coherent experience of 'the' reality. In order to visualize this line of reasoning, I have introduced a process-driven model consisting of four phases.

In the coming chapters, the idea of 'places of the imagination' and the accompanying model will be applied to, and conceptually refined by, three concrete examples. On the basis of a description of the concrete local developments

---

2 See: http://www.visitkent.co.uk/explore/ebrochures-kent-james-bond.asp [accessed: 1 December 2010].

surrounding the television detective tours in Amsterdam, Oxford and Ystad, the James Bond trip to numerous locations worldwide and the Dracula tours in Transylvania, I shall attempt to provide the foregoing theoretical explanation with flesh and blood.

PART I
TV Detectives

Chapter 3
The Guilty Landscape of the TV Detective

At the end of the afternoon, having conducted several interviews, I sank into a soft couch in the corner of the pub. I was in The White Horse, a small, rustic pub in the center of Oxford. Considering the hour, it was still calm: a few locals at the bar, chatting and sipping their flat beer, and two tables down, a couple who, considering their clothing and their luggage, were in Oxford on holiday.

The reason for my presence here was directly in front of me: The wall of the pub was covered with black and white photographs, showing scenes from the internationally popular TV detective program *Inspector Morse*. One could see the actors, John Thaw and Kevin Whateley, drinking their beer exactly here, at the very same table at which I was sitting. Everybody who has seen an episode of *Inspector Morse* – and rumour has it that around a billion people have – knows that pubs play an important role in the series. In almost every episode, Inspector Morse and his assistant Lewis stop at least once in an Oxford pub, musing about the solution to a case that appears almost unsolvable.

Most viewers notice these scenes, but nothing more. Some, however, go a step further and decide to actually visit the pub in question. Some of these are true fans, who travel oceans and continents to visit the settings of their beloved series. There are others whom one could call enthusiasts, who have occasionally seen an episode and are curious to see what the world of Morse looks like 'for real'. A special tour has been developed to address the desires of both groups: the Inspector Morse Tour. For more than ten years this tour has been one of the most popular in Oxford, attracting approximately 3,500 visitors per year.[1]

As mentioned in the preceding chapter, The Inspector Morse Tour is not a unique phenomenon. Many other cities in Europe have comparable tours or events, based specifically on the TV detective genre. For example, Ystad, a small city in the south of Sweden, was the setting for the detective series *Wallander* for a number of years, and as a result has developed into an important tourist attraction. According to the local Tourist Office, high numbers of tourists come for the semi-commercial Wallander Tour, visit the Wallander Studios, or explore 'Wallander's Ystad' on foot, using a specially-developed Wallander city map. Seen from the perspective of the local Tourist Office, Wallander has created an important opportunity for place promotion.[2]

---

1 Figures based on personal correspondence with the Oxford Tourist Information Centre.

2 Figures based on correspondence with the Ystad Tourist Office. Correspondence available for inspection on application to the author.

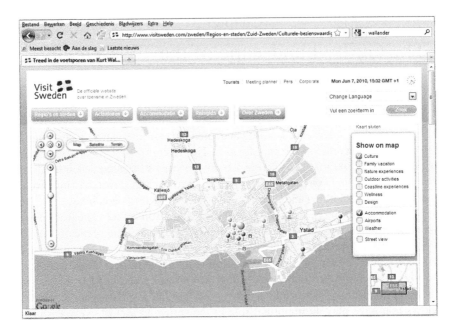

Figure 3.1   On its website Visit Sweden has a digital map of 'Wallander's Ystad'
Source: www.visitsweden.com

Similarly, Amsterdam has its own Baantjer Tour, organized by a local tourist company. During the tour, tourists are led through the historic center of Amsterdam, passing all the settings that played a role in the popular, Dutch detective series *Baantjer*. Stories from *Baantjer* are interleaved with historic accounts of actual murders and – more generally – the history of the city's famous red light district. One of the highpoints of the tour is the re-enactment of a scene from 'De Cock en het lijk aan de kerkmuur' (De Cock and the Body on the Church Wall). For this re-enactment, the organizers use a real Amsterdam street person, who plays a dead version of himself for five minutes. Tourists are invited to put on rubber gloves, take a fingerprint, and investigate the body, so that the murder of this 'authentic' victim can be solved. Every year around 3,000 tourists from the Netherlands, Belgium and France get to know the old centre of Amsterdam in this way.[3]

In some cases, instead of a permanent tour, tourists are invited for a one-off or even an annually recurring event. In October 2007, the Belgian village, Halle, organized a 'Witse Hunt', inspired by the TV detective programme *Witse*. In the neighbouring city of Ghent, the setting for the police series *Flikken*, a 'Flikken

---

3   Figures based on estimates by local guides. Correspondence available for inspection on application to the author.

Day' was organized for the tenth time. The public broadcasters, the municipality of Ghent, and local police and emergency services cooperated to produce this huge event. More than 100,000 visitors were treated to a mix of 'Flikken Games', meet-and-greets with the actors from the series, parades, street performances, and various demonstrations by the emergency services.[4]

At first sight, the themes of a television detective series – murder and death – seem difficult to reconcile with the standard assumptions of a nice day out. What is it, then, that makes the television detective so attractive as a tourist destination? What characteristics of content in a television detective series act as a trigger to prompt viewers to visit the locations where the series are recorded? This question relates to the first phase of the model described in chapter one: the phase of 'imagining'.

Our current understanding of this subject is limited to speculation (cf. Beeton 2005: 25). Thus, Cohen (1986, quoted in: Beeton 2005: 25) suggests that a film apparently only leads to tourism if the setting is clearly present in the foreground. According to Riley and Van Dooren (1992), not only does the landscape have to play a central role in the story, but the development of the protagonist also needs to be directly connected with that same landscape. Another suggestion is offered by Couldry (2000), who proposes that the popularity of the set of *Coronation Street* might be due to the fact that the series has run for a long time and that regional identity plays an important role in the plot. Last but not least, Stefan Roesch has suggested that literary precursors can be 'one of the decisive factors that might turn movies into tourism-inducing events' (Roesch 2009: 100).

Consulting studies that specifically focus on genre characteristics, in this case TV detectives, does not provide a clear answer to the questions posed above. The available work on detective fiction is limited to the historical development of the genre (Roosendaal 2002; Knight 2004; Siegel 1993; Symons 1992; Mandel 1984) and its ideological significance (Pyrhönen 1994: 81–114; Davis 2001; Gramsci 1985: 369–74; Knight 1980), in particular on the level of gender (Betz 2006; Markozwitz 2004; Munt 1994; Thomas 1995) and nationalism (Mukherjee 2003; Reitz 2004). In these studies, the importance of *place* and *localization* has remained in the shadows, with a few sporadic exceptions (Hausladen 1996; Craig 1998; McManis 1978).

Procedure

In order to find answers to the questions posed above, this chapter presents an international comparison between three popular TV detective programmes from different language regions in Europe. Selected are those TV detectives that

---

4   Figures based on official numbers from the Flikken Dag Organisation Committee. Available at: www.flikkendag.org [accessed: 30 June 2008].

have motivated the highest numbers of new tourists in their respective language regions: *Inspector Morse*, *Wallander* and *Baantjer*. Although there are tours based on other TV genres, such as comedies or dramas, this chapter is restricted to the TV detective genre. This restriction makes is possible to focus on specific genre characteristics that could motivate viewers to visit the settings.

The *Inspector Morse* series, produced by British ITV, developed an international reputation as a model of quality television. It is estimated that more than a billion people have seen one or more episodes of this series at some point (Adams 2007). In all, 33 episodes of *Inspector Morse* were made, first broadcast between 1987 and 2000. The Swedish police series *Wallander* consists of some 22 episodes, produced between 1994 and 2006, with different actors and created by different production companies. At the moment of writing, *Wallander* is especially popular in Sweden, Germany and the Netherlands, but the British adaptation of *Wallander*, broadcasted on BBC One from 2009 onwards, will perhaps also stimulate British viewers. Finally, the Dutch series *Baantjer* was produced by Endemol Productions; the 123 episodes were first broadcast between 1995 and 2006. *Baantjer* was the most-watched TV series of the past decade in the Netherlands, and it has also been broadcast in Belgium and France. Notwithstanding their differences in storyline and setting, *Inspector Morse*, *Wallander* and *Baantjer* follow the same, familiar patterns of classic detective fiction: each episode is an account of a murder investigation, whereby the viewer is gradually provided with the same clues as the detective.

Six episodes of each series were chosen at random.[5] This selection, consisting of approximately 27 hours of video, was watched in three sittings of nine hours each. A log was kept, with comments focussing on the question: How is the landscape presented and what narrative function do these pictures provide to the rest of the story? How are these representations related to the more general fields of popular and tourist culture? After the viewings, the research notes were compared in terms of differences and commonalities, leading up to the analysis by way of induction. For example: it was noted how in each episode, the detectives were repeatedly shown walking and driving through the surroundings, resulting in the category 'movement'.

---

5   The following episodes were chosen at random: from *Inspector Morse*, 'The Way through the Woods', 'The Daughters of Cain', 'Cherubim and Seraphim', 'Day of the Devil', 'Deadly Slumber', and 'Twilight of the Gods'; from *Wallander*, 'Den svaga punkten' ('The Tricksters'), Fotografen ('The Photographer'), Täckmanteln ('The Container Lorry'), Luftslottet ('The Castle Ruins'), Blodsband ('The Black King'), and Hemligheten ('The Secret'); and from *Baantjer*, 'De Cock en de moord op het bureau' ('De Cock and the Murder in the Office'), 'De Cock en de reclamemoord' ('De Cock and the Advertising Murder'), 'De Cock en de motorclubmoord' ('De Cock and the Motorcycle Club Murder'), 'De Cock en de moord in het Kremlin' ('De Cock and the Murder in the Kremlin'), 'De Cock en de moord op de wallen' ('De Cock and the Murder in the Red Light District'), and 'De Cock en de moord uit angst' ('De Cock and the Murder of Fear').

Couleur Locale

On the screen, an afternoon sky, beneath it corn fields stretching as far as the eye can see, with only a few lonely trees between the fields. Next, two children are seen bicycling down a path through a forest. They are going to an old farm, hidden in the rolling landscape. The children's voices are full of innocence, but the accompanying piano music and the neighing of a horse make the scene somehow threatening. Our expectations are fulfilled: in the dark stables, the children discover the body of the stable hand.

These are the opening shots of the *Wallander* episode 'Den svaga punkten' ('The Tricksters'). Other episodes open similarly with a wide shot, sometimes combined with a pan or tilt of the camera. We see meadows and fields stretching forever, winding country lanes, an empty beach, or dark clouds blowing in from the ocean. As depicted in Figure 3.2, the Swedish landscape plays an important role in setting the tone. Sometimes an episode starts with pictures of Ystad, the provincial town in southern Sweden that forms the setting for the *Wallander* series. These shots also have the qualities of a postcard, presenting a broad panorama, with church towers and gables of old houses poking sharply against a clear blue sky and the ocean already visible at the edge of town.

Figure 3.2   The stories in *Wallander* are set on the South Coast of Sweden
Source: Yellowbird.

The fact that each episode starts with a panoramic view of the surroundings is not unique to *Wallander*. The same occurs in the other detective programmes. This is a well-known filmic technique. Opening with a wide shot of the general surroundings, possibly combined with a *pan* (a gradual turning of the camera) introduces the viewer to the setting. Apparently, before the story can begin, it has to be situated somewhere. For example, most episodes of *Inspector Morse* open with a view of Oxford, with the ancient colleges and churches rising above the roofs of the traditional English houses. On the horizon, the gentle, rolling hills of Oxfordshire can be seen. *Baantjer* also invariably starts with a bird's eye view of Amsterdam in the early morning, with the recognizable step gables and bell gables of the old centre of Amsterdam. As a rule, these panoramic views are repeated at the end of the episode. Just before the credits appear, we see Wallander walking on the beach, or Inspector Morse going into the streets of Oxford. In fact, *Baantjer* literally ends with the same pictures as it started with, except that morning has given way to night.

The décor of the programmes is not randomly chosen, but made up of well-known icons of local identity. The bell gables on the canal houses are a *pars pro toto* of Amsterdam. The same can be said of the wide fields and wintry fir forests of southern Sweden, as well as the gardens and ancient streets and colleges of Oxford. This local atmosphere is intensified by the representation of stereotypical weather conditions: the stories of *Morse* take place under a blue sky, with an occasional English shower, while the *Wallander* series is characterized by sombre lighting, chases in the snow, and the long twilight that is so typically Scandinavian. The detective programmes thus take place in a landscape which will be familiar to most viewers, domestic as well as international (cf. Thomas 1995: 3).

What explains this recognition? According to Harvey (1973), every individual possesses a geographic imagination. Each of us carries an imaginary map of the world with us in our head, which we use to position ourselves with regard to other regions, countries, and continents. Even though we have usually not actually visited these places, we can still bring a picture of them to mind. Of course, this picture varies from person to person, but it still has a number of common sources, such as schoolbooks, novels, and – not least – popular media. Films, news broadcasts, TV series, comic books, games, current events programmes all help create an image of the world around us. Every day, billions of media users are mentally brought to places where they have never been, whether that be the Central-America of *Indiana Jones* or the Tibet of *Tintin* (cf. Crouch et al. 2005; Jansson 2002).

The strength of the geographic imagination is that it brings unity to something that in fact has no unity. There is, of course, no such single place as 'Africa' or 'Tibet'. These places are simplified to a few recognizable stereotypes, which are constantly repeated in a variety of media, thus settling into our imagination of the world. In the case of positive stereotyping, as is the case of Amsterdam, Ystad and Oxford, such a location can develop into a tourist 'must see'. Studies of tourism speak of a 'tourist gaze:' a cultivated manner of looking at landscape that is supposed to be typical of the tourist. According to Urry (2002), tourists continuously seek an image that they actually already carry with them in their heads. In this sense, the tourist is comparable to a semiotician – he or she collects and analyses images (Culler 1981; Jenkins 2003).

All three of the investigated TV detective programmes take advantage of the 'tourist gaze' of Amsterdam, Ystad and Oxford. The characterizations of the protagonists serve to further support this (cf. Lukinbeal 2005; Higson 1996; Schama 1995; Sydney-Smith 2006: 84). This is particularly clear in *Wallander*. The image of the lonely, abandoned fields of southern Sweden blend remarkably well with the character of the detective, Kurt Wallander, suffering from loneliness, a drinking problem, and a midlife crisis. When he is at his loneliest, we find him on the beach of Ystad, staring out to sea. In a similar way, the cultured, historic and academic environment of Oxford fits seamlessly with the intellectual, somewhat snobbish character of the British detective Morse.

By placing the story in a setting that is recognisable to most spectators, not only is the diagesis (the 'world' of the story) clearly demarcated, but the credibility of the series is raised across the board. The plots may be fictional, but the events could also actually have occurred – they could literally have *taken place*. This realistic setting is essential to the central theme of the investigated TV detective programmes. The moral questions concerning the dark side of interpersonal contact that arise in *Morse*, *Wallander* and *Baantjer* come into its own in a believable and recognisable setting. Of course these three detective programmes are not alone in this: the place-specific quality appears to be a common feature of the detective genre (cf. McManis 1978: 320; Cavender 1998: 87–90). In fact, the first detective story ever, written by Edgar Allen Poe (1841), was based on a 'Parisian' (though fictional) street name: *Murders in the Rue Morgue* (Goulet 2007).

Not only do the TV detective programmes reproduce the existing 'tourist gaze'; they also contribute to it at the same time. In tourism studies, following Urry (2002), much emphasis has been placed on the visual character of landscape experience. The importance of stories and other non-visual associations to the process of meaning-making has been underestimated. As Schama wrote in *Landscape and Memory* (1995), people feel attracted to specific landscapes, because these landscapes are identified with specific fantasies, stories or memories. Jeff Malpas takes a similar position in his book *Place and Experience* (1999), arguing that individuals and groups develop an image of themselves and their past on the basis of narratives, which are in turn rooted in specific spaces. In other words, people are 'topophilic' creatures: they are intrinsically bound to specific landscapes (Tuan 1974).

In the case of *Morse*, *Baantjer* and *Wallander*, many viewers will feel involved with the plot. Some may even identify themselves with the fortunes of the detectives. This personal involvement radiates off onto the locations where the programmes take place – even more so because the *couleur locale* appears to be so important to the plot, episode after episode. The landscapes that are portrayed are, as it were, 'injected' with narrative meaning. They become the focal point for processes of imagination and identification. Thus, not only do *Inspector Morse*,

Baantjer and *Wallander* confirm the established tourist gaze, but they also turn Oxford, Amsterdam and Ystad into meaningful narrative landscapes. This makes the investment in travelling to these cities doubly valuable.

On the Track

The landscape in the opening shots also plays an important role during the course of the episode. The detectives in *Inspector Morse*, *Baantjer* and *Wallander* are always on the go, travelling from suspect to police station to pub to the next suspect. We repeatedly see Morse's red Jaguar zooming through the landscape, over country roads and down lanes, on the way to the homes of suspects and witnesses. When one thinks of Inspector Morse, the image most likely to come to mind includes the detective, his assistant, his red jaguar and the historic buildings of Oxford (see Figure 3.3). The scenes in *Baantjer* and *Wallander* are almost identical. For the TV detective, the landscape is a realm that contains certain secrets, which means that it needs to be passed through and investigated, in search of truth and justice (cf. Sparks 1992: 126; Davis 2001: 137–8).

The scenes where the detectives take to the street on foot are comparable. Viewers are offered a *semi-wide shot* of the street scene: chatting students wandering through the narrow streets of Oxford with books under their arms, with a bookshop or a pub in the background. In the case of *Baantjer*, the viewer gets bicycles and trams ploughing their way through the hectic inner city of Amsterdam, passing herring sellers and window prostitutes.

The police investigation appears, in other words, as an unending movement through the narrative space (cf. Sparks 1992: 127). In this way, the TV detective programme shows a strong similarity to a certain kind of tourism. People taking a tour are also constantly on the move. They cross the landscape in hired cars, by train or by bicycle, on the way from attraction to attraction. Day trippers are of a similar order, visiting a city and spending the day wandering through the town, across squares and down lanes.

For these tourists and day trippers, the detective programme offers an ideal point of reference. They are, as it were, taken by the hand by a famous inhabitant, one who understands the local conditions and whose special powers provide access to private spaces and local secrets (cf. Tuan 1985: 57; Hills 2002: 148–9). Thus, the tourist gaze elaborates on the detective's investigative gaze (compare page 69). For example, the visitor to Ystad can obtain a map at the tourist office which lists all the locations from the *Wallander* films: places where a body was found, Wallander's favourite *konditori*, his home, and of course the police station. The *Wallander* film studios can also be visited, allowing the tourist to wander through Wallander's living room and office, or even to sit, briefly, in the inspector's chair.

By following the character's tracks meticulously, the story can be relived and at the same time supplemented with new sensory impressions. Viewers who have identified with the detectives can now follow in their footsteps. The desire

Figure 3.3   Inspector Morse and his assistant Lewis
Source: Zenith.

to be 'close' to the character seems to play an important role. For a few tourists, this desire might go one step further. An earlier study (Seaton 2002) suggested that some types of tourism present characteristics of metempsychosis: a spiritual journey, whose goal is to get into the skin of another, charismatic person, and

**Figure 3.4   The café in Ystad where Inspector Wallander enjoys his regular
cup of coffee**
Source: Photograph by Stijn Reijnders.

ultimately become one with their soul. It is not impossible that a charismatic
individual of this kind could actually be a fictional character (cf. Smith 2003;
quoted in: Karakurum 2006: 25).

The Crime Scene

As is typical for the genre of detective fiction, almost every episode of
Inspector Morse, Baantjer and *Wallander* centres around solving a murder
case. The detective work starts at the crime scene: the location where the body
was found. The detective collects clues at the scene, clues which will guide
him through the rest of the story. Such crime scenes also play an important
role in the various tours. For example, the Baantjer Tour in Amsterdam pays
considerable attention to a niche on the outside of the *Oude Zuiderkerk* (Old
South Church), where a dead street person was found in the episode 'De Cock
en het lijk tegen de Kerkmuur'. This scene is even literally re-enacted, with the
help of an Amsterdam street person who has been hired by the organization.[6]
During the Inspector Morse Tour, as well as the Wallander Tour, tourists are
taken past basements, hotel rooms and alleyways, for no other reason than that
a fictional murder case was set here. What accounts for the attraction that these
'crime scenes' exert?[7]

---

6   Hiring a street person to perform a fictional, dead street person can be labelled as
a form of 'ostension': the re-enactment or performance of stories in real life (Ellis 2001).

7   The attraction to tourists of crime scenes has been remarked on before, among
others by Rojek (1993b: 137–45) and Lennon and Foley (2000), but in these cases it always
related to *actual* murders and suicides.

Figure 3.5   **Actors Krister Henriksson and Johanna Sällström on the run during on-location shots for *Wallander***

Source: Photograph by Lars Hogsted.

At first sight, the crime scenes seem to differ too much to reach a single answer. In *Wallander*, bodies are found in the countryside: on the beach, near the harbour, or on a farmstead. In *Inspector Morse*, the murders take place in colleges or in old country houses. And finally, in *Baantjer*, the crime scenes have a much more modern, big city feel: parking garages, film studios, cellars, tunnels, and apartments. In those terms, the setting of the murder scenes differs from series to series.

However, what all these different murders have in common is the dramatic effect that takes place. The murder creates a sudden break with the everyday. The *Inspector Morse* episode 'The Daughters of Cain' provides a good example. In this episode, the spectator is first offered a stereotypical picture of Oxford: students rowing on the Thames on a lovely, summer's day. While the boats are tied up, one of the students finds a plastic bag bobbing against the shore, with the body of a grown man inside. The peaceful scene has suddenly changed into a murder scene. Compare the opening scene of the *Wallander* episode 'Täckmanteln' ('The Container Lorry'). As the daughter of Kurt Wallander walks through the woods, she exclaims: 'It's so beautiful here!' just a few minutes before she will discover a lorry full of dead bodies. Another example is shown in Figure 3.5, where we see Kurt and Linda Wallander against the background of a burning car wreck on a quiet country lane.

Setting the scene this way makes it possible to emphasize the drama of the murder. The world is turned upside down. With the arrival of the police and the coroner, the space is literally taken over. The red and white police tape cordons the murder scene off from the rest of the surroundings. With this, a crucial reversal seems to have taken place: the pastoral landscape of Oxford or Ystad (or the good-natured naughtiness of the Amsterdam landscape) suddenly becomes a 'guilty landscape'.

Guilty Landscape

The term 'guilty landscape' was introduced by the Dutch artist and writer Armando (b.1921) in the 1970s. Armando spent his youth in the vicinity of Camp Amersfoort, which served as a *Polizeiliches Durchgangslager* (Police Transit Camp) during the Second World War. What surprised Armando after the war, and what continued to influence him during his career as an artist, was the fact that this former war zone had acquired such a proper, peaceful feeling. The natural beauty was so luxuriant that it seemed impossible that murder and torture could have taken place here. But the woods around the concentration camp had witnessed horrible war crimes, and were, according to Armando accomplices. They constituted, in other words, a 'guilty landscape' (Armando 1998).

The power of the term 'guilty landscape' is that it assigns an active role to the landscape. Just like people, landscapes can harbour guilt. Of course, at first sight this appears to contradict sound reason, as the landscape is generally seen as the passive recipient, or as something that needs to be tamed. Still, when he assigns an active role to space, Armando is joining a philosophical movement that has long been part of Western thought, though it is true that it was never a dominant school. Different phenomenological philosophers, from Heidegger to Merleau-Ponty, have pointed to the importance that place has in the experience and observation of reality (Malpas 1999: 1–18). Events take place because they can find a space somewhere, and because there is a place in which the event can come to be. As Marcia Cavell (1993: 41) reasoned, even the most abstract fantasies and philosophies are never totally separate from physical reality. An event always comes into being somewhere, rooting itself 'in the only place it can, here, in the midst of things'.

Landscapes can play an active role in the way human beings experience reality, but this doesn't mean that every landscape is equally important. Some landscapes or spaces appear to be more 'active' than others. The power of a landscape clearly rises to the surface when events occur which generate negative associations. Think of old war zones, such as Camp Amersfoort, or places where major disasters or serious traffic accidents have taken place. Although the 'guilty landscape' frequently has few physical indicators that remind us of its past, the place will always retain an important, sometimes even traumatic, significance to the survivors and others who were involved (cf. Harrison 2005).

Fictional stories about gruesome murders or accidents can also make a place active. In Western folklore, there is a long tradition of legends regarding 'haunted' spaces: abandoned houses, cellars, cemeteries or lakes, which are supposed to have their own, evil force (Ellis 1989).[8] This narrative tradition reappears in literature, as well as in film and television culture (Hausladen 2000). These sorts of stories, widely known, told and remembered, contribute to making the landscape active.

In this context, the distinction between 'real' and 'fictional' stories does not seem to play such a large role. More than this, the liminality between fiction and reality appears to be precisely part of the attraction of these locations. In the case of *Baantjer*, it is worth mentioning that many of the episodes were based on actual events, which the author, Appie Baantjer, had experienced during his lengthy career as a police inspector. The Baantjer Tour pays frequent attention to the author's background, and the links between fictional and actual murder cases are continually made. It is not so much that 'reality' is brought in to emphasize the authentic character of the detective programme: there appears instead to be a reciprocal reinforcement. The real locations become more 'authentic', with the stories based on reality providing insight into it.

Conclusion

In this chapter I have attempted to find an explanation in terms of content for the popularity of the television detective tour. I have investigated which narrative characteristics of the television detective series act as a stimulus for visiting the locations. I have performed a textual analysis of three popular television series from areas with different languages in Europe, which have lead to significant tourist streams: *Baantjer*, *Inspector Morse* and *Wallander*. Comparative analysis cannot offer a comprehensive explanation of the popularity of media tours, but can certainly form the beginnings of an explanation. Besides that, it also supplements studies that already exist, in which the media content plays only a supporting role.

Based on the textual analysis, it can be concluded that the tourist attraction of the TV detective programme is due in part to the 'topophilic' character of the genre. The experience of place has a central role in detective programmes. More specifically, there are three narrative characteristics which stimulate the desire to travel. First, *couleur locale* seems to play an important role in detective programmes. In each of the investigated programmes, the opening shots locate the action in a landscape familiar to the viewer: *Baantjer* in Amsterdam's Red Light District, *Inspector Morse* in the elitist Oxford, and *Wallander* in the abandoned fields of southern Sweden. The programmes repeat icons of regional identity in

---

8   Haunted houses also have the power of attracting tourists, as the existence of various 'haunted' hotel guides shows. For example, see www.hauntedhotelguide.com for a list of haunted hotels, castles and inns in the UK.

order to raise the social-realistic content of the series. In this way, the detective programmes refer to the existing 'tourist gaze' regarding these cities, while at the same time contributing something to it. The visualized landscapes are injected with narrative meaning by the television series. This not only makes the cities of Oxford, Amsterdam and Ystad recognizable, but turns them into a meaningful landscape. A general lesson that can be gleaned from this is that narrative and visual layers of meaning are connected to each other in a more complex way than is usually supposed.

Second, the visualized landscape plays an important role in the development of each individual episode. To solve the murder cases, the inspectors in *Baantjer*, *Inspector Morse* and *Wallander* are constantly on the move. Such continuous movement through the narrative space resonates with the activities of the tourist. People on tours and day trippers are themselves on the road most of the time. For them, travel is primarily a kinaesthetic experience, based on physically moving on. Taking the TV detective as a point of departure opens up a logical means of exploring the city or region. The tourist follows in the footsteps of his or her beloved inspector, criss-crossing the local community, looking for signs and clues. The intimacy is palpable, since the inspector could, so it seems, suddenly appear around the next corner. In an extreme burst of metempsychosis, the tourist could actually become the inspector.

Finally, TV detective programmes are characterized by an obsession with the physical. Each individual episode has a crime scene as a point of departure, from which the search for clues starts. Whether in *Inspector Morse*, *Wallander* or *Baantjer*, these places are presented as everyday locations, which are suddenly transformed into a macabre counter-world by the discovery of a body. The tourist is able to visit these locations, and there, from a safe vantage point, to make the acquaintance of the guilty landscape of the TV detective: a complex junction between the diegetic world of television and the 'real' world outside.

To conclude, the locations that have been investigated represent a complex junction between the diegetic world of television and the 'real' world outside. In establishing this link, the fate of the actors also plays a role. During the Inspector Morse Tour, for example, frequent mention is made of the supposed alcoholism of the actor John Thaw, an ironic fact considering that pubs play a central role in *Inspector Morse*, which was sponsored by a brewery. In similar fashion, the personal life of Johanna Sällström, the actress who played the role of the daughter of Kurt Wallander, plays a part in the Wallander Tour. By mentioning the tragic fact of her suicide in 2007, the guide draws a link between reality and the melancholic atmosphere in *Wallander*. Such stories make the crime scenes in *Baantjer*, *Inspector Morse* and *Wallander* more than only attractive locations, simply because they are so emotionally gripping. For a moment, the tourist enters an intriguing shadowland – an area of tension between fiction and fact, between spirit and body.

Chapter 4
Doing the TV Detective Tour

In the preceding chapter the question was raised as to what makes television detectives so attractive for tourists. What can explain the drawing power of the Inspector Morse Tour in Oxford, the Baantjer Tour in Amsterdam and the Wallander Tour in Ystad? This question was answered using textual analysis: I have investigated in what way Oxford, Amsterdam and Ystad were represented in their respective series and how these representations contributed to a possible *tourist gaze*.

Although the previous chapter delivered a number of relevant results, a textual analysis can never offer a complete answer. Investigation on the spot is necessary to be able to perform a thorough analysis. With that goal in mind, in the late summer of 2007, I conducted ethnographic fieldwork during the three tours mentioned above in Oxford, Amsterdam and Ystad. City by city I have tried to map out how these tours came about, which local parties have been involved with them, how the local environment has been adapted and how these tours have been appropriated by the tourists involved. The emphasis in this chapter, therefore, lies on the *localization* of popular media narratives through specialized tours.

In total, 31 semi-structured in-depth interviews were conducted (Bryman 2004: 314–23). First, I interviewed seven guides, tourist office employees, and employees of the relevant municipal departments, all of whom had direct experience with the development and organization of the tours being investigated. These interviews focused on three main topics: design of the tour; profile of and interaction with the tourists; collaborations and conflicts with other people or organizations involved. Second, to investigate the appropriation of these tours by the tourist, I interviewed 21 tourists, selected at random during the tours; as often as possible, the interviews took place on location, immediately after the end of the tour. In the cases where this was not possible, telephone interviews were conducted later. Topics for discussion were, amongst others: motivation to participate; preparation; experience of the tour; evaluation; signifying processes. On the basis of the topics that cropped up during the interviews, I decided at a later stage to interview two local residents and a local businessperson and likewise the three original authors of the respective television series: Henning Mankell (author of *Wallander*), Colin Dexter (author of *Morse*) and Appie Baantjer (author of *Inspecteur De Cock*, filmed as *Baantjer*).

The interviews were supplemented with participatory observation during the tours, paying special attention to the structure of the tour and the behaviour of the tourists during the tour (Silverman 2002: 43–80). The transcripts that resulted

Figure 4.1   Fans of crime author Appie Baantjer congregate on the pavement outside the central library in Amsterdam on 'Baantjer Day' in 2007

Note: On the programme for the day were, among other things, guided tours around the centre of the city, demonstrations by the police, performances by ex-criminals and a musical ode to Appie Baantjer.
Source: Photograph by Judith de Leeuw.

from these interviews were extensively compared with the observation records. During this analysis, particular attention was paid to similarities between the three tours, in order to develop a more general interpretation.

Development

It is difficult to put a date on the development of places of the imagination. A TV series like *Baantjer* is already packed with recognizable pictures of the old center of Amsterdam. We can see similar images in *Inspector Morse* and *Wallander*. Each of the TV series in question builds on an existing 'tourist gaze': a cultivated way of looking at the cities Amsterdam, Oxford and Ystad, respectively (Urry 1990). More generally, these TV series follow the generic convention of representing the city as a place of ambivalence and danger (Sparks 1992: 126–7; Schmid 1995; Cavender and Bond-Mapuin 1993). By placing the story in a perspective that is recognizable to most spectators, the credibility of the series is raised across the board. The plots may be fictional, but the events could also actually have occurred – they could literally have taken place (cf. Hausladen 1996: 48–9; McManis 1978: 320).

However, each of the three associated tours does have a clear starting point at which an initiative was developed for a guided tour of the film locations of the specific TV series. Though the exact dates differ, each of these tours only came into being several years after the first season of the specific series, but generally before the end of the last season. For example, the first episode of *Inspector Morse* was broadcast in 1987, but it was not until 1996 that the Oxford Information Centre decided to develop an Inspector Morse Tour. To compare, the Baantjer Tour was developed in 2006, during *Baantjer's* ninth and last season on Dutch television. It is remarkable that the end of the TV series does not have to mean the end of the tour. Though 2000 was the last season for *Inspector Morse*, the Inspector Morse Tour is remarkably popular to this day. It is possible that the reruns on television and the distribution of the series on DVDs are partially responsible for this. Another explanation is that the TV series have fundamentally redefined the 'tourist gaze' of Amsterdam, Oxford and Ystad (cf. Bruno 2003).

The tours do not generally originate from the tourist offices, but from the tourists themselves. First, a group of enthusiastic fans approach the tourist office with a request for further information about the city where their beloved TV series takes place. In fact, the interest the fans express is not always recognized as such. The spokesperson for Wallander Film Studios in Ystad recounts:

> Early in 1992 the first people came to the tourist office and asked where [the street called] Mariagatan is. At first the tourist office didn't even realize why everyone wanted to go to Mariagatan. But of course, quite quickly we realized that it was because of Inspector Wallander [living there]. (Anna, 39, project manager, Cineteket Film Experience Centre, Ystad, Sweden)

Even after the interest is recognized as such, this does not necessarily result in an actual exploitation. In many cases, one could even speak of an initial degree of reserve. Thus, the tourist office in Ystad consciously took a reserved stance at first. On the one hand, this reflected the explicit wish of Henning Mankell, the author of the original *Wallander* book series. Mankell had publicly expressed his distaste for any kind of commercialization of his creation. On the other hand, the tourist office was also motivated by a specific marketing strategy. There were fears that promoting *Wallander* tourism too actively might lead to a one-sided perception of Ystad:

> The city of Ystad has been fairly careful. ... We have been forced to build the visitor center for film in Ystad, [but] we don't want a Disneyland. There are so many other things here is Ystad that are worthwhile promoting. We have chosen to meet the demand of the Wallander tourists, but at the same time show

them the other things that are here. (Anna, 39, project manager, Cineteket Film
Experience Centre, Ystad, Sweden)

In a similar vein, the municipality of Amsterdam is not altogether positive about
the commercial initiative associated with the Baantjer Tour. According to an
employee of the municipality, who is responsible for dealing with requests to film
in the historic center, the Baantjer Tour does not fit with the image that the city
would like to present:

> Of course the Red Light District has a very bad reputation: prostitution and
> heroin use and so on. There's activity from many sides to do everything to
> improve the image of the neighbourhood. A whole lot of the whorehouses are
> being closed, and trendy boutiques are coming in. ... If you go and organize a
> Baantjer Tour, then you get all these crazy people coming from the countryside
> to the Zeedijk ...and that just maintains the wrong image. (Ton, age unknown,
> location manager of Amsterdam City Council, the Netherlands)

The Baantjer Tour is difficult to reconcile with the municipal strategy of *place
branding*. It reinforces an existing image which the municipality would like to
get rid of, and it attracts the wrong kind of tourists – 'people from the provinces'
– instead of more sophisticated 'fashion lovers'. But in view of the fact that the
Baantjer Tour is a commercial initiative, with no special requests for streets to be
closed off or stages to be built, for example, there is little the municipality can do
but accept the tour.

It is also possible to imagine cases where the development of places of the
imagination does not proceed smoothly, actually leading to a legal conflict.
This was the case in Ystad, when the local *konditori* decided to market a special
'Wallander cake'. It was an obvious initiative: the *konditori* has an important role
in the *Wallander* stories. The café served as a place of rest, where the inspector
tried to put his thoughts in order while having a cup of coffee and a cake. Not
surprisingly, the *konditori* is a regular stop on the Wallander Tour.

Entirely in keeping with the theme of the series, the Wallander cake was
drenched in alcohol and covered with thick, police-blue icing. In this way, tourists
were invited to consume their own imagination. The author Mankell, though,
had little appreciation for this commercial appropriation of his character and
threatened to go to court if the Wallander cake was not withdrawn. The response
of the managers of the *konditori* had a marvelous simplicity. If the references to
Wallander needed to be removed from the *konditori*, then the references to the
konditori also needed to be removed from *Wallander*.

It would have been interesting to be able to analyse the results of this case, but
it was not allowed to go that far. The managers of the *konditori* wisely decided not
to fight the author in court, but found another route to get around the prohibition.
They found a family called Wallander from Stockholm who was willing to lend its

Figure 4.2   The café Fridolfs Konditorei features in *Wallander* as a trusted location where the detective could enjoy a cup of coffee.

Note: Some years ago, following the television series Fridolfs Konditorei brought out a special Wallander Cake: it is police-blue with an extra shot of alcohol. Mankell was not impressed with this blatant commercialization of his writing and sued the baker. Fridfols Konditorei suggested that if the café was no longer allowed to allude to *Wallander*, then all references to the Konditorei should be removed from the *Wallander* books.
Source: Photograph by Fredrik Ekblad.

name to the eponymous cake. Since then, a certificate on the wall of the *konditori* has confirmed their 'official' consent to the use of their name.

The disagreement may have been nipped in the bud, but it illustrates the local frictions that can be associated with the development of places of the imagination. The construction of places of the imagination is characterized by a process of appropriation, in which authors, producers, municipal authorities, city marketeers and local commercial enterprises all ascribe different meanings to these places, thereby defending their own, sometimes conflicting, interests.

Marking

In terms of their structure, the three tours that were examined show strong similarities. In all three cases, there is a guided tour, which takes around 20 tourists, lasts from one-and-a-half to two hours, and costs between 10 and 20 Euros per person. In each city, though, the means of transportation differs: in Ystad, the tourists ride in an old fire engine, in Amsterdam rental bikes are used for part of the tour, and the tour in Oxford is a walking tour. Another point of difference is the type of tourist that the tours attract. While the Baantjer Tour primarily attracts people from the Low Countries, the Inspector Morse Tour – reflecting the worldwide popularity of *Inspector Morse* – attracts a distinctly international audience. The Wallander Tour is primarily popular among Germans, Swedes, Britons, and Dutch. All three tours primarily attract white adults between 30 and 60 years old – an age group that corresponds to the traditional audience of the TV detective programs.

Around 20 sites are visited during the tours, including cafés and pubs the detectives frequented, the police station, the detective's home, and a number of crime scenes. This process of visiting numerous sites is strikingly analogous to the character of the series themselves. In *Morse, Baantjer* and *Wallander*, the detectives are also constantly on the go, moving from police station to pub to the next suspect (see preceding chapter). We could speak of a parallel 'montage' of the TV detective tour: similar locations and subsequent storylines are linked together, interrupted by short walks, thereby stimulating the imagination and creating its own notion of 'reality' (Doel and Clarke 2007; Bruno 2003). In each of the locations, the same scene is played out: the guide gestures to the tourists to stop and goes to stand with his back to the location in question. When the group has collected in front, the guide spends a couple of minutes explaining why this spot is important in the plot of the TV detective program. The location is directly linked to a specific scene from the series. While the guide is talking, the tourists listen carefully, whispering to each other, and taking photographs of the chosen object.

What kind of process is taking place here? By identifying the location as a special place – 'this is the place where …' – the location is highlighted and given a special, symbolic meaning. An everyday house suddenly becomes *the* home of Wallander. The police station in Oxford transforms into Inspector Morse's police station. And a public bar in Amsterdam instantly becomes *the* bar where Baantjer always drinks his cognac and reflects on the case he is trying to solve, while his assistant Fledder follows the passing whores with greedy eyes. By identifying the locations in this way, in the middle of the everyday street life of Ystad, Oxford and Amsterdam, imaginary entryways are opened to other, diegetic worlds. In other words, the places of the imagination are being symbolically marked.

In some cases, the places of the imagination are also literally marked. For example, the municipality of Ystad has placed various information signs in the streets of Ystad, at locations that are related to the world of *Wallander*. Thanks to these physical adjustments to the public space, 'Wallander's Ystad' is differentiated from 'the real Ystad'. The collections of photographs in the pubs reflect another form of physical marking. Thus, the visitor to Smalle Lowietje, a pub in the old Amsterdam neighborhood the Jordaan, will find a number of pictures of actors from

Figure 4.3   During the Baantjer Tour tourists pose on a bridge over the Egelantiersgracht

Note: The bridge is prominent in the opening scene of Baantjer. Kneeling in the foreground is guide Arie Blom dressed as Detective De Cock.
Source: Photograph by Stijn Reijnders.

Baantjer. In a similar way, the memory of *Inspector Morse* is honored by means of photographs and paintings on the walls of pubs such as The White Horse and The Trout Inn. This is an example of 'museumization', in which ordinary objects are taken out of their everyday context, thus receiving a new institutionalized meaning (Kirshenblatt-Gimblett 1998: 131–76).

The pub of the Randolph Hotel, a frequently used setting in *Inspector Morse*, goes one step further. A brass plaque informs visitors that they are entering the 'real' Inspector Morse bar. And thus, the pub was recently officially renamed as The Inspector Morse Bar. The brass plaque and the name change seem the definitive steps in an accelerated process of appropriation, in part encouraged by the presence of other pubs with competing claims. This competition for authenticity

Figure 4.4   Participants in the Baantjer Tour enjoying a break in the 'Smalle Lowietje', the local pub favoured by Detective De Cock

Source: Photograph by Stijn Reijnders.

between different locations has been previously identified in instances of literary tourism (Fawcett and Cormack 2001; Herbert 2001).

Once the locations have been marked in this way, the guide's spiel 'montages' them together into a meaningful network. This network of places of the imagination is, as it were, superimposed on the existing city map. Stories from the TV series are combined with information about more traditional attractions. Two related process can be identified here. On the one hand, a boundary is being constructed between the 'television world' and the 'real world'. Or as Couldry (2000) puts it, this is the boundary between what is 'inside' and what is 'outside' the media. On the other hand, the tourists are offered the possibility of transcending this boundary between the two worlds. The concrete location where this is taking place plays a central part in both of these processes.

Marking this symbolic boundary is achieved by emphasizing the differences between the two worlds. The guides are happy to point out the practical impossibility of certain scenes. 'How is it possible', the guide of the Inspector Morse Tour asks out loud, 'that Morse always found a parking space, right in front of this pub, on Oxford's busiest street?' Other popular 'bloopers' that the guides point out are impossibly short travel times or impossible routes, as well as incorrectly counted stair steps (for more on 'bloopers' see: Torchin 2002). Rather than diminishing the locations, these 'bloopers' actually emphasize the authenticity of the location compared to the authenticity of the imagination. These small differences actually serve to strengthen the reciprocity between these two worlds.

Another technique for marking this boundary is by providing details of the TV production process. For example, the guides point out camera techniques which make buildings appear larger or smaller, or locations which were rebuilt at the studio for ease of filming; they also mention the moodiness of the actors while on the set, or roads which had to be closed off for shooting. This gives the tourists a 'glimpse behind the scenes', and suggests media savvy: providing insight into the constructed nature of the media world.

Such media savvy is not just a useful, in fact necessary, tool in the current media culture, but it is a source of pleasure for many people. Tourists clearly enjoy the distinction which is made between the TV detective programs and 'the real world'. British tourist Lynda said the following about the Inspector Morse Tour:

> It's great. I really enjoyed it. You could picture scenes. And you could actually see the court and the quadrangle where he [Morse] had his heart attack. And it all looked bigger on television. I think that was interesting as well. Because when you see things on television, they look a lot bigger. And then you see them in real life, and they look smaller. I think that's television's forte. (Lynda, background unknown)

By comparing the television pictures with the actual locations in Oxford, Lynda attempts to draw a more general conclusion about the media: things on television seem to appear larger than in 'reality'.

Crossing the Line

Once a distinction has been made between the two worlds, this line is consciously crossed in a subsequent phase of the tour. A frequently used technique is to act out scenes from the TV series on location. For example, the opening scene from *Baantjer* is regularly acted out during the Baantjer Tour. This scene shows Inspector De Cock walking over a bridge in the Jordaan neighborhood, with the famous tower of the Westerkerk (Western Church) in the background. The Baantje Tour guide acts this scene out step for step – in front of the camera-ready tourists – by dressing up as Inspector De Cock and crossing the very same bridge with long, slow steps.

Tourists are also actively encouraged to step into the inspector's shoes and act out certain scenes during the tour. The re-enactment of the scene from the episode 'De Cock and the Body in the Church Wall' has already been mentioned.

Another example concerns the detectives' chairs. In Oxford as well as in
Amsterdam and in Ystad, tourists are invited to sit in the detective's chair or bar
stool. Obviously, sitting in the detective's chair is the most direct way of literally
'taking somebody's place'.

Re-enacting fictional events in a real-life setting is also known as 'ostension',
and this has a long history in Western folk culture. Folklorist Bill Ellis (2001) has
provided one of the most distinguished studies of this phenomenon. He describes
how American young people take so-called 'legend trips' to visit the locations of
established, sometimes centuries old, legends. Fixed rituals are followed, taken
from the legend itself, such as parking at a specific place in the forest, honking
the horn three times, or sitting on certain 'magical' stones. According to Ellis,
the aim of these rituals is to call up supernatural powers. Whether or not the
participants in these rituals actually believe in the story is irrelevant. The power
of ostension derives precisely from the liminal character of the event – the brief
doubt at the instant the object is touched, the fantasy which briefly leaves reason
behind, the fear which unwittingly strikes when a twig breaks somewhere in the
distance ...

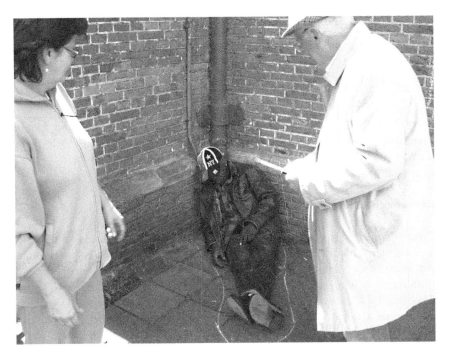

**Figure 4.5   During the Baantjer Tour a couple of scenes from *Baantjer*
are acted out with help of a hired extra, the guide is dressed as
Detective De Cock**

Source: Photograph by Stijn Reijnders.

Participants on the tours which were investigated describe a similar liminality. For example, Diana described how she had the feeling of being literally absorbed into the story during the Inspector Morse Tour:

> 'Cause we were so near, I could imagine it happening, and sort of feed in the process. It involves you in the plot. ... Now you're there, it's like you're part of the story. (Diana, background unknown)

The feeling of becoming part of the story reoccurs in other interviews, such as that of Marcus:

> It's almost like you're putting yourself into the television, isn't it? That's kind of a weird thing. ... You're going to a place inside the television almost ... to get involved inside television, and get there. (Marcus, age and occupation unknown, Ramsgate, UK)

When the tourists finally arrive in the world of television, they are not alone; rather, they have contact with a specific character: their beloved detective. Thus, Mr Malcolm described how he almost felt the presence of Morse during the Inspector Morse Tour:

> I mean, you were looking around to see whether Morse will be around the next corner, walking into the colleges or universities, like he's having a look. (Mr Malcom, age and occupation unknown, Horsely, UK)

For other tourists, such as Birgitta on the Wallander Tour, it is not so much a question of making contact as of intensifying an existing friendship:

> I thought it was very much like meeting old friends. ... You feel you know Wallander, and then you get more familiar with him. You know where he lives and you know where he was eating and drinking. It's like getting to know friends a little better. (Birgitta, background unknown)

The fact that viewers develop feelings of friendship towards a fictional character is not unique to the genre of TV detective programs. This phenomenon occurs with other genres as well. Still, the protagonists of *Wallander* and *Inspector Morse* (and to a lesser degree *Baantjer*) present certain human weaknesses, which makes it particularly easy for a certain audience segment to identify with them. Kurt Wallander and Morse are both middle-aged men, single, with a love of opera. Both of them have good deductive skills, but they are actually not cut out for their role as inspector: the gruesome crimes with which they are confronted in their line of work touch them personally, making them question the state of the country in which they were raised. To quench the melancholy and loneliness which result from these doubts, they both resort to drinking excessively. As one of the respondents mentioned:

As a police officer, he [Wallander] is a human being. He thinks a lot of the situation nearby him, but also in the world. He's a sad person. He has been married and it's been a failure. (Ewa-Gun, 55, police spokesman, Ystad, Sweden)

Many respondents recognize themselves in these characters. They are themselves middle-aged, white, middle class,[1] and they struggle with similar problems as Morse and Wallander:

We are just similar. I had also had a divorce. The guilt you feel to your children. And I had to raise them. I have worked so much some times I haven't been there for my daughters. … When it's too much for me, I grab a bottle of wine or glass of whisky and listen to opera. It's a big feeling. You can scream easier with a glass of wine. … Kurt has a lot of feelings that I like about him. He thinks about things. (Ewa-Gun, 55, police spokesman, Ystad, Sweden)

The identification with the TV detective is not only identification with a specific character, but also with the community of which this character is a part, as well as the landscape in which the character acts (cf. Lukinbeal 2005; Tuan 1985: 57). As Ana said:

I think that Kurt Wallander is very much a Swedish person as well. He is very melancholic but he is also a man in his landscape. He has got his connection to nature that lots of Swedish people have … [the] connection between Scandinavia and nature and also the detective story. (Anna, 39, project manager, Cineteket Film Experience Centre, Ystad, Sweden)

In the tourists' experience, the characters, plots and landscapes are inextricably connected to one another. By being personally present at the place where this all occurred, and by re-enacting parts of the story, the accompanying characters are called up *pars pro toto*. This would appear to be a process of *reminiscence*: recognizing details from the imagination brings forth 'new' memories. There is a clear link here to the work of Nora, in which recollection plays an important role, though the recollections of these tourists is of a much more personal, intersubjective character.

Everyday Ostension

For tourists, the experience of these places of the imagination is characterized by its liminal and temporary nature. There are, however, people for whom these places of the imagination are not tourist attractions but the everyday environment

---

1   According to Ernest Mandell (1984), crime fiction mirrors a middle-class ideology and works as an apology for the social order of bourgeois society.

Figure 4.6   Tourists wander through the film studios in Ystad where the interiors for *Wallander* were shot
Source: Photograph by Stijn Reijnders.

in which they live and work day in, day out. In this context, the police stations in Amsterdam, Ystad and Oxford are particularly noteworthy. These police stations have been, unwillingly, transformed into places of the imagination thanks to the TV detective programs. Tourists regularly come to the counter at these police stations, asking for permission to visit the office used by Morse, Baantjer or Wallander. Around town, it is not uncommon for police officers to be approached with the request to pose for a picture with Heidi from Germany or Fay from America.

Some officers object to this attention, but for the majority the skepticism transforms quite quickly into a mild pride. A police officer from Ystad tells:

> There were so many people interested in us. We felt a little bit proud. That was a very important thing, because in Sweden there is some proudness forgotten. … I think it's good for the police force of Ystad to have *Wallander*. It is public relations! (Ewa-Gun, 55, police spokesman, Ystad, Sweden)

Just as with the tourists, the police officers experience ostension, though of a more humorous nature. In this way one of the secretaries in the Ystad police station is affectionately known as 'Ebba', after the secretary in *Wallander*. There is a nameplate 'Morse' in the police station in Oxford, and two police dogs answer to the names 'Morse' and 'Lewis'. Cardboard cutouts of the inspectors often add luster to a police party in Oxford, and the author Colin Dexter is a frequent after-dinner speaker.

On some occasions, officers in Ystad discuss a case among themselves as being 'a typical Wallander':

> We had a pyromaniac three years ago. In one night he put on six buildings in fire in one and a half hours. We felt: wow! This is like in a Kurt Wallander movie. ... It was heavy. We could say this was a 'Wallander'. (Ewa-Gun, 55, police spokesman, Ystad, Sweden)

To what extent this specific case is an instance of ostension, in the formal sense of the word, depends in fact on the motivations of the pyromaniac. But in any case, the fact that his or her actions were described as such by the police shows a type of 'quasi ostension' (Ellis 1989: 202). The diegetic world of *Wallander, Inspector Morse* and *Baantjer* is not only important for tourists, but also represents an important, shared frame of reference for those who live and work among these places of the imagination.

Conclusion

The media narratives of *Wallander, Morse* and *Baantjer* are a form of popular art, which create a diegetic world. Many viewers not only want to learn about this 'other' world, but also enter this world themselves. To achieve this, they travel to Ystad, Oxford or Amsterdam, looking for physical traces of their beloved detective. They look for points of recognition amidst the everyday street life, which might serve as an entryway to another, imagined world.

Field work in Ystad, Oxford and Amsterdam indicated that the 'materiality' of the locations and the associated objects played an important role in the tourists' experience. The TV detective tours are developed around points of recognition from the detective stories, such as pubs, police stations and scenes of the crime (often alleyways and bridges). These locations were symbolically marked by the guides; the guide explained the settings and linked them to specific scenes from the detective programs. This symbolic marking was accompanied by a literal marking. Physical adjustments to streets or pub interiors served as material evidence for an imagined world. In this way, the everyday street life was subjected to a process of museumization, following the example of a popular media product. Everyday locations turned into places of the imagination.

The development of these places of the imagination was no foregone conclusion, but a process of negotiation and appropriation between various involved parties, a process which often led to discussions of authenticity. In some cases the process had a positive image effect, as in the case of the police stations of Ystad, Oxford and Amsterdam, whereas in others the process led to actual conflict, as in the row about the Wallander cake, in which the original author and a local business came into direct conflict.

The example of the Wallander cake also demonstrates the distinctively 'material' character of the tourists' performances on the locations that were studied. Tourists attempt to call up their world of imagination, by eating certain cakes at the location, by sitting on certain chairs, or by drinking certain drinks: coffee for *Wallander*, beer for *Inspector Morse*, and cognac for *Baantjer*. In fact, in Ystad special Wallander coffee cups are available, so that the experience can be repeated at home. The guides also encourage and contribute to these consumptive forms of ostension on the part of the tourists, re-enacting certain scenes from the TV series on location.

For some tourists, these activities are aimed at increasing their personal media savvy. This is achieved, for example, by considering details of the production process, which activate a process of reminiscence, or by paying attention to the various distinctions between the physical surroundings and their representation on television, such as the actual number of steps or actual travel times. But for other tourists the visit is a more intuitive experience: a temporary surrender to the imagination. By temporarily suspending their reason and giving fantasy free rein, these tourists are, briefly, on holiday in their own story.

PART II
James Bond

Chapter 5
Media Pilgrimages into the World of James Bond

In the Indian Ocean off the coast of southern Thailand lies an island that was originally known as Ko Tapu. For generations, the people of this island supported themselves by fishing, growing rice and tapping rubber. But in the middle of the 1970s, this way of life changed drastically. EON Productions – the production company responsible for the James Bond franchise – had seen the potential of the picturesque island as a location for *The Man with the Golden Gun* (1974). When this film, which was popular around the world, appeared, Ko Tapu became internationally famous almost overnight. It was particularly the shootout between James Bond and Scaramanga that nestled the island in the popular imagination (see Figure 5.1). Within a few years, Ko Tapu had become one of the top tourist attractions in Thailand, complete with James Bond tours, teeshirts and assorted souvenirs. 'James Bond Island', as it is now known, attracts over 1,000 visitors a day.

Figure 5.1 **Scene from *The Man with the Golden Gun*, shot on Ko Tapu, now often known as 'James Bond Island'**
Source: Film still from *The Man With the Golden Gun* (1974), Eon Productions.

The history of James Bond Island is not unique; there are other locations that are known entirely or partly thanks to their appearance in a James Bond film or novel. Thus Piz Gloria, a revolving restaurant in the Swiss Alps, is particularly known as the location of *On Her Majesty's Secret Service* (1969). The building still serves, 40 years on, as a Mecca for James Bond fans. Other well-known 007 locations are the casino in Monte Carlo in Monaco (*GoldenEye* and *Never Say Never Again*), Stoke Park club in Buckinghamshire (*Goldfinger* and *Tomorrow Never Dies*), the MI6 building in London (*The World is Not Enough* and others) and the beach at Laughing Waters in Jamaica (*Dr No*).

Over a period of more than four decades, 24 James Bond films have appeared, resulting in an extensive, international network of 007 locations. The tourist industry makes full use of the power of these locations to attract tourists. Visit Kent (a tourism promotion organization in the English county of Kent) has published brochures that call Kent 'James Bond Country' and state that 'Nowhere are you closer to James Bond and his creator!'. In London there are special James Bond stag parties. During these events, the prospective bridegrooms – dressed as James Bond – are offered Martinis, a speedboat trip on the Thames or an evening in a casino with their male friends.

A simple but intriguing question is, *why*? Why do people travel to places that are associated with the James Bond films and books? Part of the answer lies with Bond himself. As is well known, travel makes up a significant part of the narrative of Bond adventures. 007's missions bring him into countless world cities, deserted spots and exotic islands. Given the frequency of scenes in cars, planes and trains, one should even possibly think in terms of a kinetic aesthetic: a glorification of the phenomenon of movement. The fact is that Bond is constantly on his travels: espionage in Bond's world is no boring matter, but a dynamic lifestyle. Bond has, so to speak, a licence to travel. This tendency does not limit itself to the Bond films, but can also be observed in Fleming's novels from the 1950s and 1960s, in which travel also took on a central role. In earlier studies, it has been suggested that media products containing many depictions of travel further stimulate media pilgrimages (Tzanelli 2004: 34; cf. French: 106; see also Chapter 3 of this book). This also seems certain to have been the case with Bond.

However, Bond's lust for travel cannot by itself explain the popularity of Bond tourism. There are, of course, also enough films and novels, which are certainly popular, but do not become catalysts for comparable activities. Apparently the content of the story is not the only factor, and the socio-cultural background of the readers or viewers should also be considered along with the way in which these groups appropriate the story and the locations that go with it. As a consequence, ethnographic research into the readers and viewers is necessary.

The research into Bond tourism, however, demands a different approach to the research into the television detectives described previously. Television detective tours can be characterized by the strength of the organization that is

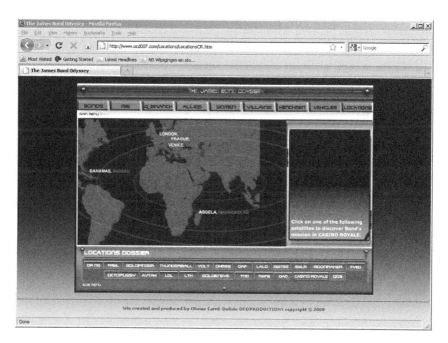

Figure 5.2   Various Internet sites offer information about the locations that were used to film the 22 James Bond films

Source: www.ocd007.com

involved: detective fans normally take part in organized trips around cities, in which a group of 20 or 30 people with the help of a guide, explore the 'Oxford of Inspector Morse' or 'Wallander's Ystad'. Bond tourism is somewhat less organized: Bond fans mostly set off on an individual basis and as a result have more say in what we have earlier called the 'localization' and 'experience' of places of the imagination.[1]

What possibly plays a role here is that the television detective series are acted out in a relatively limited space: usually in a single city with possibly some scenes in the surrounding countryside. That makes visiting television detective locations as a group feasible. The stories of James Bond are rather more dynamic: most Bond films and novels each cover several countries, if not continents, which makes organizing a tour rather more complicated and – seen from the perspective of the participants – difficult to achieve completeness. What could also possibly play a role is that Bond is the prototype of a sort of individualistic hero, who wages

---

1   It is true that there are some Bond tours available such as the 'James Bond Cab Tour' and the 'James Bond Walk' in London, or the 'James Bond Movie Site Beginners Tour' in the Bahamas (a diving tour to Bond locations under water), but overall Bond tourism is predominantly an individual affair.

war against evil on his own. This aspect of the very content of the material seems difficult to reconcile with the collective character of a tour.

However it turns out, the individual character of Bond tourism calls for an alternative approach, in which attention is not so much paid to the set up of a particular tour or to the locations, as to the perspective of the individual fan/ tourist. In order to support this theoretical perspective, in the following paragraph the concept of 'media pilgrimages' will be introduced following the work of Nick Couldry. After an explanation of the underlying theory, the concept of 'media pilgrimages' will be applied to a concrete example of Bond tourism, using a series of interviews with fans who have recently travelled to one or more Bond locations.

Media Pilgrimages

One of the most authoritative studies of media pilgrimages was based on the studio tour of the set of *Coronation Street* at Granada Studios in Manchester (Couldry 2003). According to Couldry, media pilgrimages are comparable to traditional, religious pilgrimages. He bases this interpretation on Victor and Edith Turner's classic statement (1978) that a pilgrimage is more than just a physical journey: it is also a symbolic journey towards certain central values of society. In Turner and Turner's view, building on Van Gennep (1909), media pilgrimages are characterized as a sort of retreat from everyday life, in which the pilgrims pass through three consecutive phases: first they withdraw from society, after that they operate within a finite, liminal 'anti-structure', in order finally to reintegrate reborn into society. But whereas Turner and Turner are still working in a structuralist tradition, and base their ideas on the prior existence of fundamental values underlying our society, Couldry adopts a post-structuralist approach, analysing how these rituals do not mirror but actively construct certain values.

Couldry argues that in the case of a media pilgrimage, these values are implicitly connected to the symbolic authority of the media. Thus, media pilgrimages are not only a physical journey to a location that is important in the context of a particular media story, but also represent a symbolic journey, during which the distance between the 'ordinary world' and the 'media world' is collapsed for a moment. But this entails a certain cost: making a distinction between the 'ordinary world' and the 'media world', and then creating the impression that this boundary can be crossed, albeit only briefly, reinforces and naturalizes the symbolic authority of the media. In this way, says Couldry (2003: 28), media pilgrimages function first and foremost as a 'rite of institution', reinforcing the social status of the media.

Couldry's work makes an important contribution to the study of media tourism by showing how these rituals contribute to the symbolic authority of the media. However, there are two aspects that need to be considered. Firstly, there seems to be little attention for the practical, spatial dimensions of these rituals. What these media pilgrimages may entail for the settings in question is largely left unaddressed, as is the question of what role the settings play in the 'ritual practice' of the media pilgrimage (more than just symbolizing the inside/outside boundary). This is remarkable, since space and place play such an important role in the classic, anthropological study of religious pilgrimages (Baumer 1977; Turner and Turner 1978). Pilgrimages do not just happen everywhere and anywhere; instead they acknowledge the value and authenticity of specific locations. During religious pilgrimages, specific objects from the local environment are also employed. In other words: Rituals require a concrete *Umfeld* where they can be practiced and in which they gain significance (Nissen 2000: 231–81; Post 1995). This spatial dimension of the media pilgrimage has hitherto largely remained outside the picture.

It is precisely at this point that the concept of places of the imagination can make a valuable contribution. Where the theory of media pilgrimages places the emphasis on the symbolic meaning of ritual activities – seen from the perspective of the participants – the concept of places of the imagination draws our attention to the spatial dimension and socio-cultural context in which these rituals take place. As I see it, neither concept rules the other out, but can both be incorporated at the same time into one and the same analysis. The only discrepancy between both concepts concerns the symbolic distinction that is presumed: the theory of media pilgrimages, following Couldry, is based on the symbolic distinction between those in and those outside of the media; the theory of places of the imagination rests on the notion that this distinction forms only a part of the underlying dichotomy between reality and imagination.

Secondly, his approach tends to overemphasize the role of the media. By interpreting media pilgrimages solely as rites of institution, the media are placed in a central and dominant position. To avoid this media fallacy and reduce the danger of reductionism, I think we should take into account the cultural embeddedness of media pilgrimages. In my view, this can be solved by acknowledging the way the authority of the media is related to other power structures, such as gender and ethnicity. This chapter takes the first step along that path, by focusing specifically on the relation between media pilgrimages and masculinity.

James Bond offers an ideal point of departure for analysing these gender dimensions. After all, masculinity takes a central role in the narratives of Bond. As Ian Fleming wrote in an essay (1963: 14), he created Bond for 'warm-blooded heterosexuals in railway trains, airplanes or beds'. Over the years, Bond has been the topic of many academic studies. According to the authors of these studies, James Bond is a paragon of manliness: physically strong, hard working, and in control of women and technology (Eco 1966; Bennett and Woollacott 1987; Zani 2006). The scientific literature views Bond as a unique combination of two classic male ideals: the playboy and the hard-working, self-sacrificing puritan. The female characters – the 'Bond girls' – are either traditional victims or emancipated women, who need to be 'corrected'

Figure 5.3   Several scenes from *Casino Royale* (2006) were shot in *The Ocean Club*, an existing hotel in the Bahamas

Note: For a sum of at least $1,000 per night guests can rent the room where James Bond stayed.

Source: www.jamesbondlifestyle.com

or 'reconquered' by Bond (Bennett and Woollacott 1987; but see Bold 2005). According to critics, this sexual ideology is combined with an imperialist, neo-colonial ideology: Bond travels around the world protecting the interests of the British Empire, receiving support in this from local 'boys' with a different coloured skin (Bennett and Woollacott 1987; Baron 2003; Chapman 2007: 24–9). In other words, the Bond world is an exotic, feminine landscape that needs to be roamed through and investigated, with the ultimate goal of bringing it under (Western, patriarchal) control.

The overt presence of sexual ideology in the Bond texts suggests that the theme of gender is part and parcel of media pilgrimages into the world of Bond. To put it the other way round, it is at least plausible to suppose that these media pilgrimages relate to and perhaps influence the gender identity of the people concerned. If we take into account my critical additions to Couldry's approach, this leaves us with the following question: how is the symbolic boundary between inside and outside the media in the cultural practice of Bond pilgrims related to the performance and reconstruction of dominant gender discourses from the Bond texts?

Method

Twenty-three semi-structured in-depth interviews were conducted. The respondents were recruited via a call for participants placed on eight Bond websites.[2] With the exception of one woman and one child, all the respondents were grown men; most were married and had children. The social profiles were reasonably diverse: the group contained among others civil servants, computer programmers, self-employed business people, financial experts, car dealers, journalists, teachers and accountants – professions which are traditionally associated with the (lower) middle classes. The majority of respondents came from the United States, England and the Netherlands; there were also respondents from Canada, Germany, Japan, Russia and Sweden.

What all the respondents had in common was their pronounced interest in James Bond. All of them regularly visited James Bond websites and were prepared to spend an extended period talking about their interest in Bond. Partly because the respondents came from all over the world, it was decided to conduct the interviews by phone. The interviews had a semi-structured format: although a list of questions was used, it did not dominate the interview. The respondents were given an active role in setting the tone of their interviews, so that each respondent had the chance to present his or her own perspective (Bryman 2004: 314–32). The goal of these interviews was threefold: to reconstruct the journey (How did you prepare for the journey? What did you do step by step?); to determine the inner experience of the Bond pilgrims (How did you experience being there? What made it special? What do you like about Bond?); and to discuss the overall meaning of the pilgrimage (With whom did you share your experience? How do you recall and reflect upon your journey?). In other words, although the interviews were partly aimed at gathering concrete information about the journey, the interview setting created a stage for discussing and reflecting upon the respondents' experiences. In that sense the interview method was based on a combination of 'what' and 'how' questions (Silverman 2002: 95–101). In this respect, my own travel experience and affinity with Bond stood me in good stead. I tried to motivate the respondent, without steering the interview in a particular direction.

Afterwards the draft version of this text was sent to the respondents, with the question of whether they could recognise themselves in the analysis that I had constructed. The replies to this from the respondents served not so much as a validation of the research, as a supplement to the interviews (Silverman 2002: 235–6).

The results of the interviews are presented in the following chapter. The design of the analysis is more or less based on the classic phases of the pilgrimage, in line

---

2   A call for participants was placed on the following websites in the autumn of 2008: http://commanderbond.net/; http://www.mi6.co.uk; http://www.007magazine.co.uk; http://www.jamesbondnederland.org; http://www.universalexports.net; http://www.007.info; http://www.007nl.net/cms/; and http://www.ajb007.co.uk.

with the work of Turner and Turner (1978) and Arnold van Gennep (1909). First, I describe how the Bond fans withdraw from their everyday lives in order to go and search for the world of Bond. The second, 'liminal' phase concerns those moments at which the Bond fans are actually on location. Some respondents describe this experience as 'being inside the world of Bond'. Lastly, during the 'post-liminal' phase, the Bond fans return home, where they recall and sometimes commemorate their journeys.

Chapter 6
On the Track of 007

'Earth has nothing to show more fair', wrote William Wordsworth in 1802, in praise of the view from Westminster Bridge. 'Ships, towers, domes, theatres, and temples lie/Open unto the fields, and to the sky'. More than two centuries later, the view from Westminster Bridge is still imposing, with the Palace of Westminster to the west and the London Eye to the east. To this day, the bridge is still a popular 'Kodak spot' for the never-ending stream of tourists.

But not all these tourists look at the view that Wordsworth praised: some of them lean over the bridge railing and train their eyes downwards, closely studying the pillars of the bridge. This is because in a scene from the Bond film *Die Another Day* (2002), James Bond (played by Pierce Brosnan) crosses Westminster Bridge, goes down a stairway and opens a door hidden in a pillar of the bridge. Behind the door is an abandoned underground station, where Bond finds M waiting for him with instructions for a new assignment.

The door in *Die Another Day* is a well-known literary technique, comparable to the rabbit hole in *Alice in Wonderland*, the window in *Peter Pan* or the train platform in *Harry Potter*. In all these works of fiction, the everyday, often rather boring life of the protagonist is contrasted with a rich fantasy world. The protagonist only has to open a door, accidentally fall down a rabbit hole or discover some other magical entryway to attain that other, beautiful, exciting world.

The difference between the door in *Die Another Day* and many of its literary predecessors is that this door actually exists – or rather, there is a door in one of the pillars of Westminster Bridge, it was used for the shoots in *Die Another Day* and it can still be located today. This makes the door more than just a literary technique. The place is likewise a place of the imagination: a physical point of reference to an imagined world (see Chapter 2). The fact that there is no abandoned underground station behind the door, and no secret entrance to MI6 headquarters, and that it actually leads to a broom closet, does little to reduce the attraction that this location has for James Bond fans. The fact that the door can be seen and touched is enough to justify the journey to Westminster Bridge. As Delmo said in his interview:

> Well sometimes, for example in London, you know, sometimes it is buildings that maybe Bond has been in or walked by or … I know there was a bridge where Bond entered a special door in *Die Another Day*. So I go to the bridge and pose by the door he entered, even though you could not open it, because that was only in the movie. […] So when you see it's real, then it's like: well, OK, this is a real thing that exists, not something that was a special effect or, you know, a painting or something they manufactured. (Delmo Junior, 40, unemployed, Bronx, USA)

**Figure 6.1   London has a number of locations for James Bond tourists, a
must-see is one of the doors at the foot of Westminster Bridge**

Note: In *Die Another Day* (2002) this door provided access to a disused tube station; in
reality the door leads to a small cupboard containing cleaning materials.
Source: Photograph by Stijn Reijnders.

Actually touching this door and taking a picture of it, allowed him to make Bond's
world 'more realistic' and tangible.

The quest for an imagined world is not unique to the Bond pilgrimage. In fact,
this quest is part and parcel of all media pilgrimages. In the words of Turner and
Turner (1978), every pilgrim goes through a 'pre-liminal phase' in which he/she
steps out of his/her everyday life and gains access to holy or magical locations.
As early as the literary discovery tours of the nineteenth century, which we should
regard as historical forerunners to present-day media pilgrimages, people went in
search of material traces of a literary scene (Watson 2006). What is remarkable

about Bond pilgrimages is the *way in which* these traces are investigated and described by those concerned. Where the nineteenth century readers are rumoured to have been motivated by a Romantic ideal – the re-experiencing of a piece of creativity – the James Bond fans are in fact interested in the technological aspects. For the James Bond fans, the symbolic difference between the 'normal world' and the 'world of Bond' is first and foremost a difference that needs to be traced and analysed meticulously, in an almost technological way.

This comparison is carried out to the last detail. For example, many James Bond fans work with an extensive photo collection – and this requires a degree of preparation. Before the trip, the relevant film is watched a few more times, with special attention paid to scenes filmed on location. When an identifiable location is spotted, the video or DVD is paused and the stills are printed or photographed:

> I also print out stills from the film [and] then walk around the scene. Then I go to see exactly where he [Bond] stood and so on. Then I can put the film still side by side with the actual photograph taken at the scene, so that I can notice the details more easily […] and I look at stuff like: the trees and the greenery, and notice what has grown there in the meantime. And I see that something has been broken there and that there are now more fences. (Johan, 27, construction engineer, Baarle-Nassau, the Netherlands)

Once the fan is on location, this collection of stills is compared in detail to what the fan encounters there. Pictures are taken, ideally from the same angle as in the film and under comparable weather conditions. Later, these pictures – a combination of movie stills and amateur photos – are put in folder, creating a mirror-image photo collection.

Some respondents go a step further and check complete scenes. For example, Russian respondent Vlad Pavlov compared the chase scene in *Goldeneye* (1995) with the street map of Saint Petersburg. Pavlov concluded that the scene concerned was put together from recordings in different locations, areas in the suburbs of Saint Petersburg, supplemented by props – for example a fictional statue of a horseman – and recordings from studios in London. Rather than trying to find similarities, Pavlov was looking for what are known as 'factual errors': routes and journey times that did not relate to the geographical reality of Saint Petersburg:

> Well, first of all, I live here, and I knew that there were some shots on the set, not in Saint Petersburg, and I decided: hey, let's go and pinpoint exactly, which shots are made here and there. […] I had to watch this scene several times, and I had to remember which buildings are real and then I went to those places with the screenshots printed. […] I have noticed that those scenes, those places, are not close to each other and I thought: hey, that's not real … (Vlad, 30, profession unknown, Saint Petersburg, Russia)

What is the point of this detailed plan? By paying close attention to the similarities and differences between the 'world of Bond' and the real world, the individual characteristics of both worlds are made clear.

The dichotomy between imagination and reality is not as obvious as it may at first seem. On the one hand imagination is not by definition unreal. As a rule the Bond films incorporate a high level of geographical realism, so that working out what was and what was not filmed on location, is to say the least a tricky problem. It is also a fact that films and television series do not simply imitate reality, but create their own 'reality effect' (Black 2002; Clark and Doel 2005). This certainly seems to apply to the Bond franchise: in a period of more than 40 years, tens of novels and films about Bond have created their own realistic universe following their own pattern. On the other hand, reality itself is not always unambiguous. People feel the need to acknowledge an external, univocal reality, but according to various philosophers, from George Berkeley to David Hume, it is impossible to check the existence of this simply because our sensory perception of reality is inherently subjective. Besides this cityscapes and landscapes are themselves subject to constant change: the Westminster Bridge of the present day is not the Westminster Bridge where William Wordsworth stood on the morning of 3 September 1802, nor is it the Westminster Bridge of the time when *Die Another Day* was filmed. Or in the words of the philosopher Stanley Eveling: 'An object is just a slow event' (quoted in Kirshenblatt-Gimblett 2008: 5).

In this sense 'imagination' and 'reality' are not two separate worlds. As discussed in an earlier chapter, there seems rather to be a complex and dynamic connection between many products of the imagination and real world experiences (cf. Creswell and Dixon 2002; Lukinbeal 2004; Aitken and Dixon 2006). What the James Bond fans do is to simplify this complexity and make it accessible. By traveling to the locations of the Bond films and by making a distinction between the 'world of Bond' and 'the real world', these fans discover not only an existing actual separation but also a symbolic distinction between two existing mental categories: 'imagination' and 'reality'. The power of this process originates precisely in this contrast: the mental and the symbolic are made tangible.

In addition to collecting concrete similarities and discrepancies, the respondents are also intrigued by the underlying process, namely how EON Productions uses existing locations to create a fictional world:

> And then you ask yourself when you're standing there … You really ask yourself, how in God's name did they find this? Or what made them choose this particular alley? … You start looking at totally different things – how did they make this? How does this fit together? It's more the things behind the scenes … (Martijn, 36, automotive enterpreneur, Egmond aan der Hoef, the Netherlands)

The older Bond films are especially admired, since they were made at a time when producers did not have access to advanced technology and were dependent on existing locations. The use of digital technology in the more recent films is considered a corrupting factor rather than an additional challenge:

> There's a scene from upon the hill [in which Bond is spying on Goldfinger's factory], so I got up on the hill and took photographs from exactly the same site. As opposed to lots of stunts and gadgets [nowadays], just making such a pretty straighforward scene, with a straight angle on the hill and relatively dark, it wasn't easy to shoot that! It was the 1960s! To see how it was done, I use to go there to check it out myself. (Paul, 48, stock consultant, London, UK)

The use of digital technology in more recent films is not regarded as an extra challenge but more as a contaminating factor:

> With virtual graphics and computer mediated imagery, you can pretty much make anybody, anywhere, do anything. That kind of spoils the fun of filmatography. For me, that's rubbish. I like to get up there and see how it was done – let my imagination climb up there and think about the whole technical aspects of filming those old scenes ... (Paul, 48, stock consultant, London, UK)

The interest in film technology, the making of detailed photo collections and the desire to collect and identify all the locations, together create a picture of an activity that has a strongly masculine character. The contrast with the findings of early studies of media pilgrimages among the primarily female fans of Beatrix Potter (Squire 1993, 1994) and Inspector Morse (Thomas 1995; see Chapter 4) is great. While Potter fans are eager to visit the souvenir shops – where the classic Beatrix Potter tableware brings family memories to the surface – James Bond fans hit the trail with professional camera equipment and use detailed photographic comparisons to reach authoritative conclusions about the 'reality quotient' of specific scenes.

Seen from the perspective of the Bond fans, the tracking and localizing of film locations offers the opportunity to indulge in a pursuit and to display certain masculine traits. After all, technology and rational thinking are traditionally defined as masculine realms (Connell 1995: 164–84). At the same time, these masculine traits also legitimize the pursuit itself. As is known from many fan studies, fans are often confronted with negative stereotypes of fandom: they are seen as hysterical fanatics, caught in the spell of superficial media entertainment (Hills 2002: 166–70). The same applies to Bond fans, who talk about being laughed at by friends and family members for their 'childish' hobby. By turning their media pilgrimage into a technological and rational quest for knowledge, these fans try to legitimize their hobby as a masculine thing to do.

Figure 6.2   A participant in the James Bond Tour poses in front of James Bond Island
Source: Photograph by Greg Goodman.

To the Source

Making a comparison between the 'Bond world' and the 'real world' and determining the underlying production process are not the only motivating factors for the Bond fans: many want not only to see and photograph the door from *Die Another Day*, but also to open it and enter the world that lies behind it. The respondents spoke of wanting to get 'as close as possible to the story' and to 'make a connection':

> I feel like that by actually visiting the location, it feels more real. It's like, not only have you seen it on your TV in your living room, but you have experienced it and walked in the same place ... It creates a sort of casual, realistic connection to something that already has, I guess, a fond place in my heart. (Greg, 28, businessman, New York, USA)

Actually being at the location that featured in the Bond film, and being able to see, hear, smell and feel the surroundings, makes the world of 007 tangible and close by, and brings it to life:

> And like this you get the same feeling you get when you are watching the film. And yeah, for it's really nice to ... yeah to get closer to James Bond.

[...] It feels like you are closer to that moment in the Bond film. (Johan, 27, construction engineer, Baarle-Nassau, the Netherlands)

You go to this alley or that hotel and you get some feeling. Inside you have an experience that you can not buy for money or anything. You just have to go there and get that right feeling for that moment [...] In your heart and brain you feel you have something in common ... (Gunnar, 57, car parts salesman and director of James Bond Museum, Kalmar, Sweden)

This feeling is intensified by performing certain routines at the location. Most of the respondents said that while at the location they assume a Bond pose, with their index fingers representing pistols:

It's definitely the highlight of the trip [to] at least once, you know, get a picture in a Bond-pose: put my fingers like a gun on places where James Bond was standing and take a picture. Like that. Yeah I mean ... That makes me happy. (Greg, 28, businessman, New York, USA)

By adopting this Bond pose in order to be able to take a photograph of this position using the timer on the camera, the fan's own presence in the world of Bond can be recorded and marked. (cf. Nissen 2000: 250–61).

But acting out the James Bond role is not limited to photographing certain poses. The remaining experiences of the journey were also described in a way that presents a clear analogy to the visual imagery and events in a typical Bond adventure. The respondents talked about 'tracking' and 'chasing' locations, making ready use of the knowledge of 'local informants' (almost always taxi drivers). The more prosperous respondents rent an Aston Martin and retrace the route that Bond drove in one of the films or novels. Locations that are difficult to reach, whether due to their remoteness or because access is forbidden, are seen as a particular challenge. Just like their beloved super spy, Bond fans wait for dusk and then, under the cloak of darkness, climb over that one fence or cross that one field to get close enough to take that one unique shot through a telephoto lens. In other words, Bond's spying activities are used as the ideal blueprint for organizing their own tourist activities, creating a convergence between the spy experience and the tourist experience (cf. Bratich 2009: compare page 30).

These acts of mimicry were interpreted differently among the respondents. Some respondents emphasized the hilarious and carnivalesque character of their acts. They laughed about the impersonifications and described the whole setting in notions of play. Seen from the perspective of ritual theory, these respondents can be labelled 'pretenders': participants who downplay the ritual structure and prefer to celebrate the loose and playful elements of the ritual (Rooijakkers 2000: 190–94). It is striking that in this case, the one and only female respondent positioned herself as a 'pretender' *pur sang*:

> It was only sort of a joke [...] We used the James Bond activities as a loose
> direction. [...] So for us it wasn't, erm, too obsessive, it was more quirky fun
> things that we could do in our day. (Victoria, 42, management assistant at a non-
> profit organization, Vancouver, Canada)

Other respondents – the so-called 'believers' – emphasized the more serious
elements of these acts of mimicry. They liked to talk about the deeper meanings
they attached to their involvement, echoing notions from Clifford Geertz' work on
'deep play' (Geertz 1972). Through their mimetic proceedings, these respondents
aim to 'bring Bond to life'. They talked about the feeling of having entered this
'other' world, if only temporarily:

> It's like a kick, you know. You're at least here, now. You're on the same track. ...
> You're not just watching it, but you are inside the film. (Nils, 51, civil servant,
> Sweden)

These experiences seem to comply with the characteristics of the liminal phase
of a ritual, as described in the works of Turner and Turner (1978) and Van
Gennep (1909). This is the phase in which the Bond pilgrims are the furthest
from their everyday lives and momentarily seem to merge into an 'anti-structure',
experiencing oceanic feelings of freedom.

But as established in the previous chapter, this 'anti-structure' does not stand
apart from a socio-cultural context. What appears to be the case from historical
and empirical studies is that it is true that participants in pilgrimages experience
a feeling of community, but that this feeling is grounded in certain group values
which also play a role in the 'normal world' (Taylor 2004). Likewise, historian
Dorothea French has shown that the pilgrimage to 'Saint Patrick's Purgatory'
in the west of Ireland, popular in the fourteenth and fifteenth centuries, was an
opportunity exclusive to people from the higher social groups. At the heart of this
pilgrimage lay the ideologies of militarism and male dominance – values that were
of core importance in a period notable for wars and crusades (French 1994).

Thus, the question arises: what values form the basis of the Bond pilgrimages?
In the first instance, the interviews suggest that there is no single answer to this
question. Bond's moral world seems to vary from respondent to respondent. To
his fans, James Bond is first and foremost an 'open' character, which allows each
fan to give his/her own interpretation (cf. Bennett and Woollacott 1987). Still, a
number of values recurred in the interviews. Ideas of manliness are central to most
respondents' view of Bond. He is seen as a 'strong' and 'brave' man, who is able
to surround himself with fast cars, weapons and beautiful women. Bond is 'good
at what he does' and lives an 'independent life':

> He's very good in what he does, and you get motivated, I think, when you're
> watching James Bond films. Because you need to be so lucky to be like him.
> I mean he does ... He's not afraid of anything. [...] It's his courageness, his

dominant braveness ... And he's independent: he never has to do anything other than what he really wants. He has the strong will to live a good life. (Anders, 36, working at a television production company, Sweden)

This perception of Bond's character agrees with previous studies that have looked at the sexual ideology of James Bond. Scholars interpret Bond as a paragon of manliness – a paragon with a strongly conservative and hetero-normative disposition (Chancellor 2005: 79–83). The respondents recognize this sexual ideology, but without explicitly condemning it. On the contrary, these fans – the majority of whom are white, heterosexual men – adore the character of Bond. Exploring his world and repeating some of his actions affords these fans the opportunity to embody and act out a certain idealized masculinity:

A license to be what you like. That is part of the fun. Fantasy and fun are involved, [but it's also about] the emulation you put in your life. Thinking this particular way, dressing that way, enjoying the items, the cars ... (Paul, 48, stock consultant, London, UK)

By performing Bond, these fans perform and thereby reconstruct a specific masculinity (cf. Buchbinder 1998; Edley and Wetherell 1995). Of course, this kind of gender performance comes with a price. In everyday life, at work or at home, a totally different kind of masculinity is often expected. In his book *Masculinities* (1995), Robert William Connell describes how men in contemporary societies are confronted with a role model of masculinity that is hard to live up to. On television and in films they are presented with the picture that they need to be sexy, powerful, smart and strong, all at the same time. According to Connell, many men have difficulty reconciling this 'hegemonic masculinity' with the social position they occupy in the context of family, friends and work. Elaborating on Connell's work, some authors have spoken of finding a balance between an 'imagined masculinity' and 'lived reality' (e.g. Beynon 2002: 64–8).

The Bond locations occupy a special position in this difficult balancing act. They provide the respondents with an opportunity to physically embody an imagined masculinity – if only briefly. What makes these experiences meaningful is their physical nature. As Henri Lefebvre (1991) argued, every ideology needs a geophysical foundation, where individual power relations can be physically delineated. In line with Lefebvre, one could speak of the Bond locations as material-symbolic sources of masculinity, where the individual's sexual identity can be rediscovered, delineated and reinforced (cf. Wezel 1998: 247).

Despite this, everyday life is often less far away than one would think, even at these liminal landscapes of Bond. This is certainly the case of respondents who combine their Bond pilgrimage with a normal holiday with their partner. They need to adjust their desire to those of their spouse:

Figure 6.3   There are more than a dozen James Bond networks active on the Internet

Note: One of the subjects discussed on these forums is the locations of the films and novels.
Source: www.commanderbond.net

Look, I need to plan things a bit with my partner. The first thing is she doesn't care about James Bond, not one bit … She always thinks I'm crazy… When we visit Bond locations, there's also something … uh …'cul-tu-ral' or something like that to see. I mean, then we can visit James Bond locations one day and then we can go shopping for the next four days. (Johan, 27, construction engineer, Baarle-Nassau, the Netherlands)

Places of Memory

Once they are home, the pictures are combined to create the previously-mentioned mirror-image photo albums, generally complemented with written travel accounts. In most cases, these accounts are posted on one of the many James Bond fan websites. As Gary said in his interview, fans like to 'brag to those who care'. By sharing their travel experiences with others (primarily other male Bond fans), they are able to demonstrate their status as connoisseur in a society of like-minded fans, thus creating 'fan cultural capital' (Fiske 1992):

You've been doing this for years. After a while, of course, a lot of people start to think of you as sort of an expert in that area. I really want to be able to show that in one way or another. (Martijn, 36, automotive enterpreneur, Egmond aan der Hoef, the Netherlands)

These travel accounts also serve more personal purposes. Many respondents talked about regularly going through all the photos and reviving their memories. Having being present at the scene and having acted out certain poses or scenes has not only brought the film to life, but has also brought back memories that are related to the film. It is, in other words, a process of reminiscence – of retrieving 'forgotten' memories by repeating actions from the past. Just as singing old songs from one's schooldays can rekindle one's memories of those days, visiting locations that feature in Bond films can bring back memories that are attached to early viewing experiences.

This process does not appear to the same degree for all Bond films: the first encounter with the Bond phenomenon takes pride of place. The respondents gave extensive descriptions of how they went to the cinema, usually as boys in their early teens, to see their first Bond film:

Obviously I've been a Bond fan since I was a kid. I saw my first James Bond film when I was nine. That was *Goldfinger* [...] I'd say *Goldfinger* probably made the biggest impact on me. In the car, hopping on the Aston Martin, being a young boy, made it a big thing for me. It all started with that. (Paul, 48, stock consultant, London, UK)

Someone who repeatedly crops up in these stories is the father of the respondent. Various respondents described how, when they were young, they were taken by their father to their first Bond film. Why is this memory so important and why did it play such an unexpectedly large part in the interviews? One possible explanation is that the respondents experienced this as an important moment, which in a symbolic way marked their own masculinity. That is, after all, not inaccurate: a boy, exactly at the time of his life in which he is discovering his own masculinity, is taken by his father to enter for the first time the diegetic world of the hypermasculine Bond with the concomitant doses of sex and violence. This all takes place in a space which, in itself, constitutes a moratorium from everyday life: in the darkness of the cinema's auditorium, time seems to stand still and daily life seems miles away.

This hypothesis might at first sight seem somewhat far-fetched, but that this sort of initiation ritual is not strange within the world of the Bond fan may also become apparent from the existence of the James Bond stag parties mentioned above. Stag parties are pre-eminently an initiation ritual, in which the passage from bachelor to married man is recorded and celebrated. Although these parties normally occur at a different time of life to the first visit to the cinema to see a Bond film in the company of one's father, both these rites of passage make up part of the same rite – the ritual steps that are taken in the passage of life in modern manhood.[1]

Travelling to the locations from that film – 20, 30 or even 40 years later – brings back memories from that period of the respondent's youth, and also brings to mind the symbolic distinction between the boy and the man:

> When you get older, you get more sheltered. But there is a bit of boyishness left. Dressing that way, enjoying the items, car and gadgets [recaptures] a bit of boyishness. Being a boy again ... (Paul, 48, stock consultant, London, UK)

A temporary return to the dreams of youth permits a fresh look at the present:

> When I was growing up, that was the kind of things I aspired to: I wanted to drive a really nice car, I wanted to go on holidays to exotic locations. For me he [Bond] just got absolutely everything that a boy growing up in the 1970s and 1980s, you know, would aspire to be like. [Now] I can do all the things I want to do. Live the James Bond lifestyle because I've worked hard, you know, integrated by the number of professional qualifications. That was my inspiration behind wanting to go. ... To do the things that he has done, even when you know it's in a fictional world. (Gary, 48, profession unknown, London, UK)

These quotations present an experiential world in which the symbolic distinction between boy and man is linked to a dichotomy between imagination and reality. Although it is not always expressed so explicitly, this experience is common to many of the other respondents. Many people view childhood as a period full of fantasy, but one that is closed, in sharp contrast to the grown-up man's world in which career and social competition take first place. Visiting Bond locations appears to offer respondents a progressive experience: first, the dichotomies are identified on the basis of a detailed comparison; second, this affords them the possibility of transcending these dichotomies, so that the imagination can rule, if only briefly, within the restrictions of the adult world. In other words: for these men, Bond makes fantasizing a legitimate activity.

Of course, this process of reminiscence leads not only to autobiographically oriented recollections. Another kind of memory can also be evoked. Sometimes, for example, James Bond's past is recalled. One of the respondents tells, for example, of how he imitated a photograph of George Lazenby in London: hanging from a lamppost with Big Ben in the background. From his point of view the photograph represents 'a memorable moment from the history of James

---

1   Ian Fleming wrote his first Bond novel *Casino Royale* in the winter of 1952, two months before his marriage to Ann Charteris, who was pregnant at the time. According to Henry Chancellor (2005), Fleming used the act of writing *Casino Royale* as a way of taking leave of his own bachelor life.

Bond', namely the introduction of a new actor after years of faithful service from Sean Connery.

Other memories are of a more general, historical character. The Bond films serve as important time-documents for many fans. Their memories of the 1960s are inextricably linked with the imagery in films like *From Russia with Love* (1963) and *On Her Majesty's Secret Service* (1969). Visiting these Bond locations now in 2009 makes them aware of the passage of time:

> When you're at the spot, you can see what things have changed since the 1960s and 1970s. … Things have really changed, you know. (Nils, 51, civil servant, Sweden)

By being present on location and comparing the current landscape with the old film stills, the respondents can see what has changed over the years – not only in themselves and in Bond, but also in the wider cultural landscape of which they and Bond are part.

Figure 6.4   The James Bond Museum in Keswick, England

Note: This museum's collection consists mainly of the cars which, rumour has it, were used in the shooting of the James Bond films.
Source: Photograph by Stijn Reijnders.

Figure 6.5   The James Bond Museum in Nybro, Sweden

Note: In the foreground is museum director and James Bond fan, Gunnar. Apart from cars, Gunnar's collection also contains various pieces of fan memorabilia, such as posters, computer games, clothing, props, board games, cigarette lighters, watches and model cars.

Source: Photograph by Stijn Reijnders.

Conclusion

In 1953, James Bond made his first trip to the French Riviera with the assignment to beat the Russian spy Le Chiffre at the Casino Royale. Since then, Bond has travelled the world with regularity. Many of these locations have developed into tourist hot-spots. As tourists follow in Bond's footsteps, the common processes of commoditization and commercialization have accompanied them. In some cases one can speak of a short-lived hype – a period of two or three years in which the locations are literally inundated with tourists. Other locations retain their attractive power and develop over the years into regular destinations for a band of faithful Bond fans. So far, it is largely unknown which factors play the determining role in this process. Other questions also remain unanswered, such as what effects this wave of tourists has on the local community, or what the future of this type of tourism will be.

This chapter focused on the perspective of the tourists, by reconstructing and analysing their experience of the Bond pilgrimage. Previous studies have shown the importance of the symbolic difference between 'inside' and 'outside' the media for the experience of media pilgrimages. Media pilgrimages are said to support the symbolic authority of the media; by honouring locations from the media, one honours the media as an institution.

From the 23 interviews with Bond fans, it appears that the Bond pilgrimage confirms the importance of this symbolic difference. During the Bond pilgrimage, the differences between everyday life and the world of Bond are carefully traced and analysed; this is followed by a temporary and carnivalesque transgression of this inside/outside border. Some respondents emphasized the ludicrous elements of these acts, while others appeared to take the Bond pilgrimage much more seriously. However, both groups acknowledge the importance of the above-mentioned symbolic difference.

At the same time, this symbolic difference cannot be seen apart from the underlying theme of masculinity that runs through all the phases of the Bond pilgrimage. For example, Bond fans described the pre-liminal phase – in which pilgrims leave their everyday lives and approach their destinations – in highly technological and rational terms. For them, the confrontation between 'inside' and 'outside' the media is primarily a technologically driven enterprise, focused on gathering photographic 'evidence' and identifying the 'reality quotient' of specific scenes. Comparing the world of Bond with the 'real world' offers them the possibility to perform certain masculine traits, while, vice versa, these masculine characteristics also legitimize the pilgrimage as a whole, in line with the fans' attempts to counter dominant stereotypes of 'fanatic' and 'childish' fans.

The liminal phase is focused on bringing Bond 'to life'. The respondents – overwhelmingly white, middle-aged, heterosexual men – talked about temporarily 'going into' the world of Bond. This process is encouraged by performing certain mimetic actions, such as assuming a Bond pose, taking the same route as Bond did or performing complete scenes. They admire Bond for his decisiveness and his wanderlust, and view him as a model of masculinity. By walking in the footsteps of 007, the respondents repeat and re-experience the narrative development, and are able to sneak inside James Bond for a moment. For them, the Bond world serves as a place where they can portray and embody an idealized masculinity, namely the 'mediated masculinity' of Bond.

Lastly, in the post-liminal phase, the Bond fans return home and record their experiences in mirror-image photo collections – iconic interpretations of the real/reel dichotomy. Some fans decide to upload their collections to one of the many websites for James Bond fans in order to share their experiences with like-minded people, primarily other male Bond fans. By showing their photographs and commenting on the technological skills of the production team, these fans consolidate their status and authority. Having the final say about the 'truth' of a certain scene or production detail is indeed a valuable trait in the James Bond fan hierarchy.

Thus, although the symbolic difference between 'inside' and 'outside' the media plays a structuring role in the proceedings of the Bond pilgrimage, viewed from the perspective of the fans, this inside/outside dichotomy is inseparably intertwined with notions of masculinity. When it comes to the point, the former functions as a ritual set of instruments for the latter. By tracing, analysing and finally transgressing the symbolic boundary between everyday life and the world of Bond, these fans are able to experience a Turnerian 'anti-structure', a moratorium on everyday life, in the company of an imagined hero. Mimicking Bond at the very place where he was sitting, running, fighting or making love, enables them to recollect the roots of their own masculinity, to refresh it and to define it.

More in general, these conclusions show the importance of analysing media pilgrimages in a wider cultural context. The authority of the media does not come about in a vacuum, but is tightly interwoven with other power configurations. In addition to gender, dimensions of class and ethnicity will also need to be explored in further research. Equally important are those media pilgrimages that seem to subvert existing power configurations. While the Bond pilgrimage tends to reconstruct patriarchal notions of masculinity, other media pilgrimages might actually challenge these values, operating as Bondian 'counterspies'. The concept of media pilgrimage, placed in its proper cultural context, promises to be a valuable tool in analysing these processes.

PART III
Dracula

Chapter 7
Stalking the Count

One of the conclusions of the previous chapter was that visits to James Bond locations exhibit two apparently opposite characteristics. On the one hand the visitors make a very rational, almost technocratic comparison between the geophysical environment and the images from the films. On the other hand they are in search of a way in which to reconcile this contrast between reality and imagination, so that they themselves can, for a short time, be part of an alternative, more glamorous or fast-moving world. In the forthcoming chapter, I shall investigate whether this dichotomy also applies to Dracula fans and if so, what general conclusions can be drawn from this about experiencing and giving meaning to places of the imagination.

Figure 7.1   Bram Stoker set the castle of Count Dracula in the Borgo Pass, a pass in the Carpathian mountains in Romania

Note: In Stoker's time, there wasn't actually a castle at this location. Nor is anything known about a similar castle in the time of Vlad Dracula. However, a century after the publication of *Dracula*, a large castle hotel was built in the Borgo Pass, based on Stoker's descriptions. The Dracula Castle Hotel is nowadays a permanent feature of various Dracula tours.
Source: Photograph by Stijn Reijnders.

Beyond the Forest

One of the most attractive passages of Bram Stoker's novel _Dracula_ (1897) describes how the bookkeeper Jonathan Harker travels through Transylvania. Journeying by train and by stagecoach, he passes through a country of endless forests and mist-shrouded hills, on an assignment to provide advice to a certain Count Dracula. The descriptions of Harker's journey are so thrilling and visual that they have acquired a permanent place in the popular imagination, thanks in part to the many reprints of the novel but also the innumerable screen versions that appeared throughout the twentieth century. For many people, Transylvania, which is currently a province of Romania, has become synonymous with the Dracula Country: a land of howling wolves, vampires, bats, and gloomy castles. In the popular imagination, Transylvania is not only on the geographic periphery of Europe, but also on its mental periphery – a kingdom where superstitions and ancient rituals are still widespread (Andras 1999; Light 2007: 749; Walker and Wright 1997).

For a long time, the Romanian government had trouble accepting this perception. During the Communist period (1945–1989), in particular, associations with Dracula were avoided as much as possible. The stereotype of a superstitious and primitive hinterland was hard to reconcile with the image of a progressive utopian state that the Communist Party wished to present to the world (Light 2007; Muresan and Smith 1998). Partly for this reason, for many years there was no Romanian translation of _Dracula_ available. Despite this internal opposition, as early as the 1970s, a growing stream of foreign tourists began to visit the country, specifically interested in locations from the novel. Stoker's description of Harker's journey is both detailed and geographically well-informed, which made it possible for these tourists to repeat large parts of the journey step by step. And where Stoker's descriptions provided insufficient detail, the tourists were happy to fill in the gaps themselves.

A good example of this is the search for Count Dracula's castle. Stoker placed the castle in a remote location in the north of Transylvania, an area where no castle originally stood. Eager to at least find a castle, the tourists found Bran Castle, several hundred kilometres to the south. The fact that this was not the 'authentic' location was perhaps a disadvantage, but Bran Castle was in a location that was easy for the tourists to reach, and its restored Gothic style was a good fit with the image tourists had of what Dracula's castle should look like. And so, Dracula fans appropriated Bran Castle as 'their' castle – with foreign tour operators following on their heels.

Today Bran Castle is actually one of the tourist highlights of the region and, despite the dubious nature of the claim, is widely known as _the_ Dracula Castle, with all the associated teeshirts, mugs, ashtrays and other Dracula souvenirs (Light 2007: 752–5). More generally, Dracula is still the flagship of the Romanian tourist industry. Many Romanians don't think so much of the bloodthirsty count – they regard the story as a piece of coarse stereotyping of

Romanian history and identity – but find it necessary for financial reasons to play the Dracula card.[1]

A simple, but nevertheless intriguing, question is 'Why?' Why do Dracula fans feel the need to associate their cherished story with specific, identifiable locations, even when this is, in fact, impossible based on the information provided in the story, and when, as in the case of Romania, the host country provides little encouragement? What significance do they subsequently give to their visit? It is remarkable that this sort of question seldom crops up in existing studies of Dracula. Various manuscripts and edited books have been written on the Dracula phenomenon and a *Journal of Dracula Studies* has even existed since 1999, but the connection with tourism rarely appears in these studies – with a couple of exceptions (Arata 1990; Walker and Wright 1997; Muresan and Smith 1998; Light 2007; Hovi 2008).

In order to address this, I performed a study of two different groups of Dracula tourists in 2009. The first group was composed of a party of American tourists who took the 'Dracula Tour' in July 2009. Just one of the many Dracula tours offered in Romania, this seven-day bus tour visits various Dracula sites around the country. The trip started in Bucharest and went via Bran Castle and the mediaeval town of Brasov to the renowned Dracula Hotel in Piatra Fantanele, and returned via the town of Sibiu and the ruins of Poenari Castle.[2] The second group was composed of members of the Dracula Society, a British association of fans of Bram Stoker's *Dracula*. In September 2009, the Dracula Society organised a literary walking tour of Whitby, a town on the English coast where several chapters of Dracula are set. Participatory observations were made during both events, and in-depth interviews were conducted. After a short description of the background to these tours, and the methods of research, there will follow an analysis of the fieldwork.

---

1 Unfortunately there are few figures available about the precise extent of Dracula tourism. Evidence for this is only anecdotal. Therefore in 1998, a number of interviews were conducted among foreign visitors to Bran castle – one of the tourist highlights in Transylvania. All 63 interviewees said that they were already familiar with the story of Dracula before their visit and with the detail that Transylvania was Dracula's home (Muresan and Smith 1998: 83). The question of whether Dracula was actually one of their reasons for visiting Romania in the first place was, however, not answered in this study. Another indication as to the popularity of Dracula tourism can be found in the considerable number of Dracula tours on offer. See for example: http://www.dractours. com; http://www.dracula-tour.com; http://www.mysteriousjourneys.com; http://www. adventuretransylvania.com/halloween-dracula.htm; http://www.culturalromtour.com/ trip_special-trips-complete-dracula-tour_15.html; http://touromania.50webs.com/tour-dracula.html; http://www.vakantie-roemenie.com/dracula-reis.html. Regular travel guides such as the Lonely Planet also give significant amounts of space to the Dracula myth in the descriptions of Romania, see for example: http://www.lonelyplanet.com/ romania [all sites accessed: 6 February 2010].

2 For a more comprehensive description of the route, see: http://www.dractours.com/ itinerary.htm.

Figure 7.2   The 'Dracula Experience' in Whitby, England

Note: This attaction offers visitors a walking tour through the story of Dracula, using a rather archaic setting with waxwork figures and appropriate sound and light effects.
Source: Photograph by Stijn Reijnders.

Lovers of Dracula

The Dracula Tour has been offered since 1999 by ITE, an American travel agency specialised in so-called 'terror tours'. In addition to the Dracula Tour, ITE offers 'GhosTours' of England and Scotland, and an annual 'Weekend of the Witch' in Salem, Massachusetts, the town infamous for its seventeenth-century witch hunts. The Dracula Tour is offered twice a year, in the summer and around Halloween. In total, the two tours attract around 100 tourists a year, primarily Americans of different age groups (between 18 and 70 years old), with a relatively large proportion of students, teachers and retirees. On average, a quarter of the participants are traveling alone, while the remaining three quarters have booked together. These are not necessarily couples; for example, this summer, two sisters (Anne-Marie and Monica) and a father and son (John and Jonas) were traveling together. The American Dracula tourists are often recognizable from their dark clothing and teeshirts with the names of hard rock bands or Gothic-related texts. Approximately half of the group said they are part of, or have affinity with, the Gothic subculture.[3]

Secondly, research was conducted during a meeting of the Dracula Society in Whitby. This association was founded in 1973, with the stated goal of providing a platform for 'lovers of the Vampire and his Kind'. The association currently has about 100 members, primarily adult Britons between 30 and 60 years old, most of them working in the service sector, as civil servants, archivists, librarians, teachers or administrative assistants. In addition to regular evening meetings with discussions, lectures or film showings, the Dracula Society also organizes trips and holidays, generally to visit locations associated with the work of Stoker or other authors of the nineteenth century Gothic genre. In 2009, among other things, the Society planned a weekend in Whitby. The high point of the weekend was an hour and a half literary walking tour of the old town centre of this North English seaside town, following in the steps of the characters Lucy and Mina Harker. As far as their dress, these British Dracula tourists were less outspoken than their American counterparts; still, a certain affinity for the Gothic subculture could be observed here as well.

Two methods were applied during the field study: in-depth interviews and participatory observation. The in-depth interviews took place during or after the tour. The structure of the Dracula Tour was well-suited to on-the-spot interviews: there was enough time during the bus journeys to conduct complete interviews. During the literary walking tour of Whitby, the possibility of interviewing participants was truly limited; for this reason, discussions during the walk were purely exploratory, introducing the project, and the actual interviews were conducted later by telephone. In all, 21 tourists were interviewed.

The interviews were set up in a semi-structured manner. Certain questions were determined in advance, but the list was not followed in any absolute way. The respondents were given the opportunity to introduce their own subjects and perspectives, as long as these had some relevance to the central topic: the

---

3   Participation in a Dracula tour is also regularly combined with a honeymoon. In earlier years several newly-weds reenacted their recently performed marriage ceremony during the costume dinner at the Dracula Castle Hotel, obviously something of a deviation from the official ceremony. During the summer tour of 2009, there were, sadly, no 'wedding ceremonies'.

Figure 7.3   It is not only Dracula locations which are visited during the Dracula tour, but also other 'dark' locations such as graveyards and torture chambers

Source: Photograph by Stijn Reijnders.

experience of Dracula tourism. The interviews with tourists were structured under three thematic headings: motivation (e.g., How long have you been interested in Dracula? Why did you decide to take this trip?); experiences (e.g., What does it feel like to be in Dracula Country? What makes this trip interesting?); and meaning (e.g., Has this trip changed your attitude towards Dracula? What is different now that you have been here?). Later, each interview was transcribed word for word (Bryman 2004: 314–23).

Participatory observation was conducted to complement the interviews. This observation focused on three aspects:

1. The tour's geographical structure (departure point, route, destination);
2. The techniques the guides used to structure the tour (introducing, marking the places, placing them in context, concluding); and
3. The tourists' behaviour (reactions to the guide, contact with the surroundings, ritual behaviours). Notes were recorded in a logbook during the observation (Silverman 2002: 43–80; Bryman 2004: 289–311).

After the tours, the transcripts and logbooks were thoroughly compared. First, similarities were sought, as these can indicate general, common structures. Then, special attention was paid to striking differences and exceptions to the rule, keeping our eyes open for the diversity and inner dynamics of the phenomenon of media tourism. Not only were the differences between individual tourists considered, but also the difference that sprung from the medium or the structure of the tour. After all, the literary walking tour has a completely different cultural-historical background than the bus tour, and it also produces a different experience of the landscape (cf. Plate 2006).

During the analysis of these interviews and observations, it became apparent that the inner experience of the Dracula tourist – similar to that of the Bond tourist – is characterised by the dynamic between two, partially opposing, modes. While Dracula tourists use rational terms to describe their desire to make concrete comparisons between imagination and reality, they are also driven by an emotional longing for those two worlds to converge. What these two modes have in common is their distinctly physical foundation: they are both based on a sensory experience of the local environment. In the following paragraphs, both processes shall be described and analysed in turn, with the aim of finally coming to a synthesis in the conclusion.

Figure 7.4   Participants in the Dracula literary walking tour through Whitby pause by a bench that is dedicated to Bram Stoker

Note: From this bench the walker can enjoy a panoramic view of Whitby and can follow an important passage from the book literally step by step.

Source: Photograph by Stijn Reijnders.

Tracing the Imagination

On a bright, sunny day, West Cliff, on the coast of North Yorkshire, presents the tourist with a majestic panorama. Down below is the historic harbour town of Whitby, with its narrow lanes and characteristic red roofs. And beyond that, East Cliff rises tens of meters above the town, topped with the ruins of an abbey, the parish church and its graveyard.

For aficionados of *Dracula*, this is more than just a picturesque panorama. The landscape that is displayed before their eyes is also recognizable as the setting of a particular chapter from Stoker's *Dracula*. This is the scene where Lucy wakes up in the night and – drawn by some unknown force – runs through the town in her white nightgown, climbs up the cliff by a staircase carved into the cliffside, to reach the graveyard above the town, where she surrenders herself to Count Dracula among the tombstones.

For the Dracula fans, their visit to Whitby is, in a certain sense, not their first encounter with the town, but rather a renewed encounter, the realization of a journey which they have already taken many times in their imagination. Most of the participants of the literary walking tour have been Dracula fans for many years (as have their American counterparts on the Dracula Tour in Romania). They have read and reread the novel, they regularly watch Dracula films, and they devour any information that has anything to do with Bram Stoker, vampires, or gothic fiction in general. Their years of fascination with Dracula means that most Dracula fans have developed a deep familiarity, not only with the story and its characters, but also with the landscape associated with the story. In their imagination, Dracula Country has practically taken physical form:

> I was really young when I got this thought into my head. … Since I was a little kid this is where I wanted to be … There are places as a child that I always wanted to be and this is the main one here. (Rebecka, 35, housewife, Florida, USA), Dracula Tour

The question remains what ultimately motivated the fans to go one step further and actually go on the journey, booking a trip to Whitby or Transylvania. The interviews show that the exact motives vary from individual to individual. Still, when asked for their reasons, most of the respondents mentioned that at a certain moment they had the thought that perhaps Dracula was more than just imagination. For example, they discovered that Transylvania is the name of a real province in Romania and that there really is a town on the north coast of England called Whitby. Another reason that was frequently mentioned was discovering information about Count Dracula's castle. Precisely these kinds of concrete objects and buildings can develop into tactile references to an imagined universe:

Ever since I found out that he had a castle in Romania, I wanted to go there. [...] Since then, I've always wanted to go there, all my life. (Jason, 38, civil servant, London), Whitby Walk

In this regard, it is not so strange that Dracula has motivated so many fans. In his novel, Bram Stoker paid a remarkable amount of attention to creating a realistic setting (Walker and Wright 1997). From the perspective of the novel, this topographic realism has an evident narrative function: by setting *Dracula* in a believable environment, Stoker hoped to give the supernatural events in the story a degree of believability. For the Dracula tourist more than a century later, this topographical realism provides a completely different advantage: the original novel and the later film versions provide numerous references that help the tourist to identify Dracula Country.

Figure 7.5   Bram Stoker set the castle of Count Dracula in a location where originally there was no castle

Note: In their desire to find a castle anyway, tourists in the 1970s began to look at Bran Castle, which was not only conveniently located in the tourist infrastructure but also looked like something out of a Disney fairy-tale. Since then, Bran Castle has become known as 'the' castle of Dracula and a visit to the castle is now a permanent feature of every Dracula tour.

Source: Photograph by Stijn Reijnders.

In fact, a similar process takes place for the Dracula tourists as was the case with Stoker, though the process is reversed. While Stoker used existing surroundings and local history to create his story, the Dracula tourists take the story itself as their point of departure, proceeding to search for signs of reality in the story. The Dracula films and the book are carefully sifted for information: references to existing place names are checked, the travel routes described are traced on the map, and departure and arrival times are compared with official travel times, preferably historical sources from the late nineteenth century. In this way, fans anchor Dracula Country in topographic and historical reality:

> It's like trying to work out something from clues. ... To try to work out where these things would be. Where was Carfax? Where was the asylum, as it says in the book? ... We do not know [for sure], but it is certainly interesting to speculate on all these things. (Dave, 66, retired, London, UK), Whitby Walk

Obviously, not all Dracula fans are equally ardent in this pursuit. Finding reality in fiction is, in theory, a never-ending activity. One fan will put more energy into this than another; some fans become truly caught up in the research and sleuthing that is involved. On top of this, it is clear that fans accumulate a degree of knowledge over time. There are many different individuals, associations and organizations around the world which are devoted to studying everything that is associated with Dracula. This Dracula fan culture has existed for many decades, but since the spread of the Internet in the 1990s it has truly taken off. In the year 2010, potential Dracula tourists have an extensive digital archive at their disposal, with background information, travel accounts, academic studies, and commercial travel offers. In this sense, the contemporary Dracula tourist is not only following in the footsteps of Count Dracula, but also of earlier fans – the 'scouts' in the 1970s and the following generations of Dracula fans.

Once there, in Dracula Country, the rational analytic mode remains dominant, at least at first. Dracula fans see visiting places of the imagination first and foremost as an ideal opportunity to gather more information, in order to substantiate the 'truth' behind the story:

> To visit the location is to see if the picture is ... Well, if it corresponds in any way to the reality of it. ... That's what attracted me to Whitby. (Alan, 51, civil servant from Berkshire, UK), Whitby Walk

An important part of this process is establishing factual errors: precisely those parts of the story which do *not* correspond with the physical, spatial environment. For example, it is common to check certain travel times and routes on location. During a previous visit to Whitby, members of the Dracula Society re-enacted Lucy's nocturnal walk, with one of the female members of the society running through the historic centre of Whitby, complete with hair streaming, and wearing a white nightgown. One of the conclusions from this re-enactment was that Stoker didn't take the presence of Church Street into account: in Stoker's *Dracula,* Lucy runs across the bridge and immediately climbs the 199 steps that go up to the graveyard, but in the test it appeared that there is a considerable distance between the bridge and the stairs.

The historical context of Dracula is also subjected to detailed investigation. During both of the tours, the events in the story are thoroughly compared with the historical background of the respective locations. This comparison takes a particularly prominent role in the Dracula Tour. The Romanian guide Radu Cruceru makes a point of emphasizing that, contrary to what many foreign tourists like to imagine, Count Dracula is not the same as Vlad Dracula, the fifteenth-century Wallachian prince. For Radu, just as for many Romanians, it is still hard to accept that foreign tourists associate their own national hero with a common, blood-sucking vampire from the horror genre. There is something bitter for Romanians in general that their beautiful but relatively poor country depends to a certain degree on a type of tourism based – in their view – on a negative

Figure 7.6   The Dracula Tour consists of a seven-day bus journey through Romania, visiting various locations which have some connection with Stoker's novel, the later film shoots or the life of Vlad Dracula

Note: The Romanian guide, Radu Cruceru, emphasises in his stories the difference between the ficticious Count Dracula and the historical figure Vlad Dracula, a difference that carries little importance for the tourists.

Source: Photograph by Stijn Reijnders.

stereotype of Romanian history and identity (Light 2007: 755–9; Muresan and Smith 1998: 76).

Though the guide does pay attention to Dracula, he solves this symbolic conflict between economic interests and national pride by continually pointing out the many differences between Dracula and the historical 'reality'. In practice this leads to a situation where history is employed for an authoritative treatise about what is 'real' and especially what is 'unreal' about Dracula.[4]

How do the Dracula tourists respond to such a critical approach? The interviews show that they react in different ways. Inasmuch as the historical reality agrees with the story of Dracula, most of the tourists are immediately interested. These points of agreement are seen as an important validation of the historical 'reality' of Dracula:

> The fantastical bits become more plausible because they are rooted in historical fact. (Alan, 51, civil servant, Berkshire, UK), Whitby Walk

> It gives it more reality, quite simply. You know, it gives it a more of a real feeling. ... It makes the experience more of a reality. (John, 58, profession unknown, Chicago, USA), Dracula Tour

In her interview, Zelia (a 28 year-old female from London, studying at a teacher training college) explained that the historical background made the story 'more real, rather than just sort of a book'. For Jason (a 38 year-old civil servant from London) the background also made the story 'more believable'. And for James (a 28 year-old student from Ontario) the historical background is more than just validation, but also a way of deepening the imagination by adding to the original story:

> When you see and hear that stuff you can, you know, I can imagine also a lot of things around it where the story should be. (James, 28, student, Ontario, USA), Dracula Tour

Even when the story of Dracula clearly departs from historical reality, this does not pose a problem for all the fans. On the contrary, some of them warmly welcome this division of fact and fiction:

> [I like] ... being in the country and hearing the actual history and finding out what is actually Hollywood and made up. To just hear the actual history behind it. To learn more of the truth behind it. (James, 28, student, Ontario, USA), Dracula Tour

---

4 Conversely it could also be argued that the comparison between imagination and history leads precisely to a validation of the latter. By comparing it with the 'not real' and 'false' character of imagination, emphasis is also placed on history's 'realness' – a quality which by no means goes without saying in these post-structuralist times.

For fans like James, the distinction between 'actual history' and 'Hollywood' serves as a variant of the previously mentioned factual errors – tangible 'evidence' of the underlying dichotomy between reality and imagination.

Other fans are less receptive to questioning the historical basis of Dracula. For them, historical reality becomes a direct threat to the world of the imagination – an attack on the fantastical palace that they have built and cherished over the years:

> My whole life I really thought that there were vampires out there and I needed to go find them. And now that I've come here and heard that Vlad Tempest isn't … The whole vampire theory is kind of shot. … To realize that he is just 'The Impaler' and not an actual vampire … He didn't bite anybody's neck, he just cut their heads off. Which is still good, but it's different. (Rebecka, 35, housewife, Florida, USA), Dracula Tour

Earlier in this chapter, I suggested that visiting places of the imagination can serve to enrich the imagination. But as the last quote shows, these kind of additions are not necessarily positive; for some fans they can also lead to a process of demystification.

Similarly, in their interviews, both Julia (a 57 year-old librarian from London) and Dave (a 66 year-old retired man from London) commented that while a rational comparison of imagination and reality is certainly interesting, it should not be taken too far:

> There are members of our Dracula Society [who] examine places and descriptions and timetables to access their accuracy or not. To me I think … it's an interesting exercise, but it's missing the point. … They don't have to match. … It's almost like cataloguing something – it kind of takes away its magic, if you try to do it too much. … I'd rather just have hints or suggestions. (Julia, 57, librarian London, UK), Whitby Walk

Following Samuel Taylor Coleridge (1817), the consumption of fiction can indeed be defined as the 'suspension of disbelief', the willingness to accept the world of the imagination as real. Readers put their critical, generalized world view aside for the time being, in order to be able to surrender themselves to a particular story. Fans like Rebecca and Julia seem to experience media tourism as an extension of this 'suspension of disbelief' – a tool which allows them to renew and, at least temporarily, extend their belief in the imaginary beyond the confines of the book or film. Superfluous information about the historical 'inaccuracies' of Dracula can, however, easily ruin this desire.

The Resurrection of Dracula

While making a rational comparison of reality and imagination may be an interesting activity for many Dracula tourists, it does not represent the essential

Figure 7.7   The highlight of the Dracula Tour is the fancy-dress party
Note: This is held in the cellar of the Dracula Castle Hotel. At the end of the evening, prizes
are awarded for the best costume and sexiest outfit.
Source: Photograph by Pepijn Dros.

goal of their trip. Instead, many emphasize that they travelled to Whitby or
Transylvania with the intention of deepening their emotional connection with the
story. In practice, female respondents emphasized this slightly more often than
their male counterparts. Still, this emotional mode is certainly not sex specific.
What is, in fact, striking is that both approaches are regularly mentioned, by men
as well as women, and by British as well as American fans. In many cases, both
modes were even mentioned in one and the same interview. Respondents described
how they would continually shift from a rational investigation of the environment
to a more emotional, affective stance.

Both modes are based on a tangible experience of the local environment. Being
right there, present at the location, rather than experiencing it at a distance via the
media, is always central to their experience. But while the rational mode is first
and foremost associated with a visual experience, a far broader range of senses is
addressed in the emotional mode:

> I get inspired after I see something or I read something. … For me, the natural
> extension is to come to the actual place … to experience and to see it, to breathe
> it and to taste it, in a way you can't on the pages of a book or on the pictures on a

screen. I wanted more. I didn't want to watch it on a two-dimensional screen or read it in black and white. I wanted to drink it all in. (Jonas, 33, teacher, Chicago, USA), Dracula Tour

By drinking in Dracula Country, by smelling it, feeling it, seeing it and tasting it, the fans get a livelier and more complete picture; the respondents talk about getting the sense that they have come 'closer to the story'. Other respondents describe how being at the location gave them the feeling that they were making a 'connection':

It is not so much that you are reading something, which is a separate thing from you. [Being there] you can almost imagine yourself being in the novel, a sort of bystander in the novel. (Alan, 51, civil servant, Berkshire, UK), Whitby Walk

The boundary between imagination and reality, which was just so precisely identified and delineated in the previous phase, is now temporarily suspended instead. Dracula Country has come alive, and the tourists are themselves, if temporarily, guests there:

Going there and seeing it for yourself puts you in the story as well. (Zelia, 28, teacher in training, London, UK), Whitby Walk

This whole tour is kind of becoming a character in the novel. ... Once you land in Transylvania and we're going through you really do feel like a character in the story, specifically Jonathan Harker. ... This is about the closest I can get to actually living out one of my favourite stories. (Jonas, 33, teacher, Chicago, USA), Dracula Tour

Identifying with the story and the characters in this way also has an erotic aspect. For example, several female respondents described the pronounced sexual attraction that Count Dracula exercises. Male respondents specifically emphasized that they identified with the power Dracula has over women. During the interviews, this glamorization of Count Dracula flowed effortlessly into a description of his violent character:

There's parts of women that wants more of ... aggressive too, like behind closed doors and like Dracula is kind of this like, charmer and everything and seducer. But then he's, you know, with the biting, it's almost more like a rough type of ... taking, yeah. So many things are based around blood like with sanguin, religion, stuff like that. Like ... It's a sexy thing. (Tanja, 29, computer trainer, South Beach, USA), Dracula Tour

Dracula tourists such as Tanya are attracted by the story of Dracula, partly because of its dark-romantic mix of eroticism and violence. This theme was clearly already present in the original work of Bram Stoker, but became even more pronounced in recent filmic adaptations such as Francis Ford Coppola's *Dracula* (1992) (e.g., Griffin 1980; McGrath 1997). Of course, this macabre theme does not limit itself only to Dracula but is a more general characteristic of the Gothic genre as well as of the Gothic sub-culture with which, as already stated, a number of the respondents identify (Botting 2008: 3–4; Hodkinson 2002: 43–6). In spite of this, the story of Dracula can certainly be seen as one of the first and most appealing exponents of this theme (cf. Griffin 1980; McGrath 1997).

This erotic dimension of the Dracula phenomenon acquires a strikingly physical character during the Dracula Tour. Being there in person on location, able to experience the possible closeness of Count Dracula, stimulates both excitement and a mild fear. One's own body is moving in and through Dracula Country, and one is exposed to all the potential risks of this place. This explains why the inner experience of the Dracula tourist is first and foremost a sensual pleasure – a pleasure that is only possible because it takes place far from home, far from America and London, in the liminal twilight of Transylvania or Whitby.

This excitement is reinforced by re-enacting certain episodes from the story on location, such as spending a night in the same hotel as Jonathan Harker or having the same evening meal ('robber steak') as Stoker described in the book. While not everybody participates equally actively in this – the British members of the Dracula Society being, for example, somewhat more reserved in this regard – such re-enactments represent an essential part of many Dracula tourists' experience.

Perhaps one of the most striking examples is the night spent in the Dracula Castle Hotel, built more or less on the 'authentic' location on Borgo Pass, which is a regular feature of the Dracula Tour. A fancy-dress ball is organized each year during the stay, and the traveling companions dress up as Count Dracula, vampires, night nurses, the dead, or other similar characters, ideally with deep *décolleté* and tight leather clothing. The costumed tourists spend the evening with music, food and drink, all in the décor of the so-called 'catacombs' of the Dracula Castle. Around midnight, the party descends into the crypts of the castle, where the coffin of Count Dracula awaits them. One by one the tourists take their place in the coffin, the one with a cheery smile, the other clearly frightened. The party continues until two or three in the morning, but after this 'official' portion, various fans continue the party in their hotel rooms – thereby feeding the breakfast rumours about 'X-rated Dracula viewings' and possibly even 'biting sessions' among fellow tourists.

Of course, such re-enactments are by no means unique to Dracula. This phenomenon, where fans re-enact episodes from stories, is also known as 'ostention'. In one of the most authoritative studies in this field, the American folklorist Bill Ellis (1989, 2001) describes how since at least the nineteenth century American young people have organised so-called legend trips to the locations of specific stories or legends. In general these are mysterious stories of murder and manslaughter, whether true or based on rumour, taking place in isolated houses, in railway viaducts or beside remote lakes. At these locations, ritual routines are performed, such as calling someone's name or re-enacting the events in the story, with the intention of calling these characters back to life.

One wonders whether the Dracula fans actually believe in Count Dracula's existence at the moment that they call his name. The majority of respondents denied this during their interviews. Those who did claim to believe in vampires justified their belief on the basis of rational, pseudo-scientific arguments. One

Figure 7.8 **Two party-goers have prepared a sketch in which the remaining participants in the Dracula tour are likened to characters from Stoker's novel, the coach party become, as it were, 'fictionalised'**

Source: Photograph by Pepijn Dros.

frequently mentioned argument was the fact that there are known medical cases of people who regularly need blood transfusions.

But, as Ellis would argue, it doesn't in fact matter whether the Dracula fans actually believe in vampires or not. What is important is the suggestion which these procedures make – namely the idea that it could actually be possible, that vampires might indeed wander the Transylvanian nights, with Count Dracula at their head. This suggestion, made in a striking environment far from home, with like-minded companions is of itself enough to generate the necessary frisson.

In this way, the trip becomes a true re-experiencing of the story, complete with the excitement and unease that was so characteristic of the first reading or viewing experience – an excitement which is maintained in Stoker's novel to the very last page. It is just like in the story: the Dracula tourist can actually only breathe easily at the end of the journey, when the Count is finally defeated and the hero returns home:

> When I go back that first night and I sleep in my bed I will be able to curl up and be safe in my bed, [back] from the wilds of Transylvania. Boy, if this Dracula was a real guy and I was going in Jonathan Harker's footsteps, you know, here I am safe and happy. (Jonas, 33, teacher, Chicago, USA), Dracula Tour

Figure 7.9   At around midnight the party-goers from the Dracula tour can take their places one-by-one in the tomb of Count Dracula, hidden in the catacombs of the Dracula Castle Hotel

Source: Photograph by Pepijn Dros.

Conclusion

More than a century after the publication of *Dracula* (1897), its eponymous main character still exercises a mysterious attraction on readers. Large numbers of tourists travel to Transylvania every year, in search of traces of the Count. They are inspired by the novel itself, or by one of the many film versions, some of which have become classics of the genre. They are members of literary associations or fan clubs, or they come as individuals. They are students as well as retired people, men as well as women. What attracts them to Transylvania or one of the other locations associated with this vampire story? And what meaning do they ultimately attribute to the trip?

This chapter has attempted to find answers to these questions. On the basis of an analysis of interviews with Dracula tourists, as well as participatory observation during two Dracula tours, several conclusions can be drawn. The tourists do indeed have different motives and they employ different processes to give meaning to the experience, and similarly, certain differences of emphasis were found between men and women and between American tourists and British ones; but most striking are the many similarities. There would appear to be such a thing as *the* inner experience of the Dracula tourist. This inner experience is characterised by a specific dynamics: the tension between two partially contradictory modes.

On the one hand, the Dracula tourist is driven by the desire to make a concrete comparison between the landscape they are visiting and the picture they have created of that landscape based on the book or the Dracula films. This motivation is widely encouraged by the topographic-realistic elements in the story. For example, it is common for the Dracula tourist to encounter information about the 'real' Dracula castle. The tourist then searches further, assisted by the many publications and websites dealing with the subject, and traces all the steps that are taken by Jonathan Harker, Count Dracula, and the other characters. They can discover concrete place names or names of regions, but the more fanatical Dracula tourists also work out complete journey routes, considering travel times and descriptions of the climate. So doing, they trace Dracula Country and anchor it in the topographical reality.

Such treatment gradually leads to the wish to go there in person. By personally visiting the locations from the book and films, fans hope they can penetrate the 'truth' behind the story. They do this by comparing the spatial descriptions that Stoker made and the visual representations from the films with the physical reality of the actual environment. This comparison of imagination and reality is continued on a temporal level, by comparing Stoker's *Dracula* with the local history, in particular the life history of Vlad Dracula. It is primarily the Romanian guides who use history as an authoritative argument about what is 'real' and 'unreal' about Dracula. The Dracula tourists welcome this information insofar as it shows historical parallels between reality and Dracula; they view these parallels as providing important validation to the story. Discrepancies produce more varied reactions: some fans see historic 'corrections' of the story as a satisfying and enriching addition, while others consider this a direct assault on their imagination, as the demystification of a cherished world.

On the other hand, the rational approach of tracing and making comparisons contrasts with a more intuitive, emotional experience of these places of the imagination. The Dracula tourists describe the desire to come 'closer to the story' and to make a 'connection' through a symbiosis between reality and imagination. They reach this by ceasing to pay so much attention to details, but instead experiencing the environment in its totality – to taste, see, hear, feel and smell it – in order to experience the story anew thanks to these sensory stimuli. These sensory experiences also have an indisputably erotic dimension, in which the tourist puts his or her own body in the proximity of Count Dracula, who is known both for his sexual attraction and for his violent character. The story is even sometimes literally brought to life. Fans re-enact certain scenes, sleep in the same hotels as the characters, and eat the same meals as the characters in the book. These re-enactments serve as the basis of a liminal experience, in which fans have the sense that they are summoning Count Dracula and are personally becoming part of the story.

These two modes have been described and analysed separately, but in practice they have a certain mutual dependence. It is only possible to come 'closer' to the story once it is clear where the story takes place, and once the location has been 'validated'. By first tracing and marking the symbolic boundary between imagination and reality, this boundary can, in a later stage, be crossed. In this regard, it would seem that one can speak of a certain anti-rational dynamics: while first there is the need to test the imagination against reality, one subsequently has the desire to remove the distinction between imagination and reality in order to temporarily become a part of another, more exciting world.

Further study is needed to determine whether this anti-rational dynamics is typical for Dracula tourists in particular, or whether it applies to media tourism in general. Of course, it is striking that Stoker's original novel also contains a strong element of anti-rationalism. The hunt for Count Dracula, which forms a leitmotif of the novel and later films, is built up around the tension between scientific knowledge and supernatural phenomena, which are not easily captured by such knowledge; this tension is personified in the story by the character of the Dutch scientist Van Helsing. At first glance, these similarities in content would appear to argue that the results of the Dracula study have a limited generalizability. Other characteristics of Dracula tourism, such as the strong emphasis on physicality and the attention to topographic realism, would also appear to have a direct connection with this specific story.

On the other hand, it was apparent from the research into James Bond and the television detective tours that one could recognize a comparable contradiction among these fans/tourists – notwithstanding the huge differences in narrative between the three examples in question. In that respect, the bipolar tension between on the one hand wanting to discern and establish a separation and on the other hand wanting to believe in an alternative reality, seems to be a general symptom of media tourism. With this problem we touch on the material for the final chapter, in which the conclusions drawn from the individual sections of research shall be put together in order to come to more general conclusions by means of comparison.

Chapter 8
Conclusion: The Magic of Imagining

In the summer of 2010, three years after the start of this research project, I found myself once more in Oxford. The reason for my presence there was the new Harry Potter tour: a walking tour through the centre of Oxford to the locations that had been used for the books and films about this apprentice wizard. The Harry Potter tour was not the only media-related attraction in Oxford; tourists could now choose between an Alice in Wonderland tour, a Literary tour, a Tolkien tour or an Oxford Film Sites tour.

Despite the increase in competition from other media tours, the Inspector Morse Tour also seemed to be enjoying enduring popularity. Every day, scores of Morse fans were still wandering past the pubs, houses and crime scenes which were connected with the eponymous television detective and his successor Lewis. Once again the same serene silence set in at the moment that the party arrived at the lawn of Exeter College.

That tourists would stand in awed silence at the spot where a much-loved fictional personality collapsed with a heart attack, had at first astonished me. Now, at the end of the research project, astonishment has given way to recognition. The world seems to be full of comparable 'magic' places, which perhaps to the outsider mean nothing, but which for the initiated have a special meaning and have a connection with particular stories, which are very close to their hearts. These are the ubiquitous *lieux d'imagination* (places of the imagination): symbolic-material references to a world of the imagination.

Imagination and Religion

Earlier studies have alluded to the supposedly religious character of this form of tourism. The analogy between media tours and religious pilgrimages is indeed striking: just as pilgrims travel to places which have a sacred meaning for them – normally because a miracle has occurred there or it is the resting place for the tangible remains of some holy person – so fans make their journeys to the locations of film or television recordings, in the hope of picking up the trail of their much-loved characters. The religious miracles are replaced by marvellous stories of superheroes, vampire hunters and detectives but the essence remains the same: both cases concern stories about charismatic characters who are embroiled in a struggle against Evil. And somewhere in the world, lie the relics – physical remains – which commemorate this struggle, whether they take the form of a lawn (Morse), a tomb (Dracula) or, in the case of Bond, a blood-

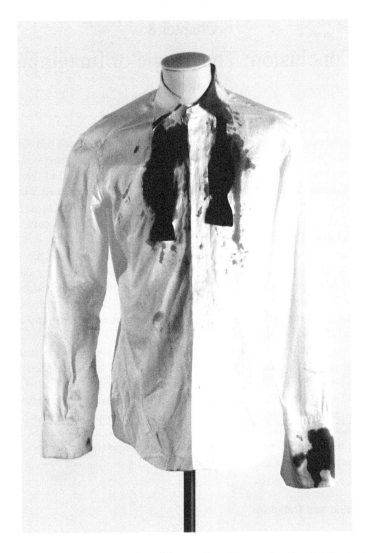

**Figure 8.1   The bloodied shirt of James Bond, worn by Daniel Craig during
                the filming of Casino Royale**

Source: Danjaq, LLC United Artists Corp, Columbia Pictures.

stained shirt, as depicted in Figure 8.1. This shirt, worn by Daniel Craig during
the filming of Casino Royale, was displayed in April 2008 at the Imperial War
Museum in London as part the exhibition on James Bond and Ian Fleming: *For
Your Eyes Only*.

However, it would be a step too far to talk of a complete similarity between
religious pilgrimages and the phenomenon of media tourism. Equating religion to

fiction does not do justice to the essential difference between the two phenomena that those involved experience. Many of the people I spoke to in the interviews felt themselves to be strongly involved in the stories,[1] but their relationship with them was ultimately characterized by a suspension of disbelief. They surrendered themselves willingly to the power of their imagination, but this abandonment at all times played itself out within clear boundaries. What above all made media tourism attractive for them was precisely the underlying contrast between imagination and reality – the symbolic crossing of the border between two qualities. It can be properly assumed that the attitude of religious pilgrims is fundamentally different: most of them operate under the assumption of an underlying Truth, which they believe in.

Besides this is the question of whether pilgrimages and media tourism ultimately fulfill a comparable function. From a historical perspective, religious pilgrimages have always had differing goals: people went out of religious conviction, for the companionship or for recreation or for penance (in the past, people convicted of crimes could, in some cases, mitigate their sentence if they went on a pilgrimage). Today pilgrimages still fulfill various functions, but what has become increasingly important is the supposed healing power of pilgrimages. Anyone who has visited the cave at Lourdes can vouch for this: the cave is visited by a constant stream of invalids and the elderly, walking on crutches or sitting in wheelchairs, and even patients lying in hospital beds are not an infrequent sight. In media tourism elements of healing are scarce. As became apparent in the analysis of Bond tourism earlier in this book, Bond locations for some fans serve as a symbolic-material source of masculinity, where they can immerse themselves in the 'mediated masculinity' of Bond. But strictly speaking this seems to appeal not so much to a desire to be healed but to a longing for *male rejuvenation*.

To resume, in my view the comparison between religion and media tourism is somewhat unfortunate, because it puts two things on a par with each other, which are fundamentally different. In a certain sense the comparison itself is misleading: it makes the unknown (media tourism) *apparently familiar* by putting it together with the known (the pilgrimage).

That said, there is unmistakable recognition of a definite structural analogy between media tourism and the pilgrimage. Both phenomena clearly have a number of common characteristics. In my view, however, this cannot be explained by seeing the one as a contemporary variant of the other, but by interpreting both phenomena as the externalization of an underlying need. What people in both cases strive for is to *make tangible* that which is not tangible in the first place. By coupling imagination or religion (both being complex imaginary systems) to specific locations and material objects, something that is fundamentally

---

1 For some tourists, media tours serve only as a practical stepping-stone – a recognizable starting point for getting to know a new city or region. However this clearly applies only to a minority; the majority of tourists who were interviewed for this project, spoke of having a strong bond with the films, books or television series concerned.

immaterial can be pinned down, appropriated and consumed. In this sense, eating a Wallander cake is comparable to receiving the consecrated host: people give form to an abstract idea (to paraphrase Plato), in order subsequently to take it literally inside themselves. This is, as it were, a magical act, centred around the fundamental boundary between the bodily and the spiritual. By making the spiritual material and consuming it, so the belief goes, part of its power can be appropriated.

This book was directed specifically at media tourism: the act of visiting locations which are connected with popular media narratives. However, the urge to make something tangible out of what is intangible seems to be somewhat more widespread in contemporary popular culture. Think, for example, of the graves of media celebrities, which can exert an enormous power of attraction on fans. Memorable examples of this are the grave of Jim Morrison in Père-Lachaise or the tomb of Elvis Presley in Graceland. This attracts more than half a million visitors a year and was even chosen a few years ago as a 'national landmark'. Celebrities of this stature have been all but inaccessible during their lifetimes, but now fans can stand just six feet from the remains of their hero. Another example is the active trade in the clothing, utensils and garbage of celebrities on websites like Ebay.com (Britney Spears' spat out chewing gum fetches prices of up to $14,000). In this sense, there seems to be a commonly felt need for *proximity*: people want to be literally close to the stars and the stories which they have grown up with. It could be suggested that this need for proximity implicitly betrays a feeling of *distance* – a yawning chasm between what is experienced as the world in the media and the world outside of it. To the extent that the influence of the media on our world becomes stronger, it seems that non-mediated experiences acquire a more and more unique character.

But with these general conclusions we are getting ahead of ourselves. First it is our task to lay out the results of this research. What was researched in this book is how making the intangible tangible is formalized in the actual practice of media tourism. Three examples were investigated: television detective tours; James Bond trips and Dracula tours. On the basis of fieldwork in, among other places Amsterdam, Oxford, Ystad, Jamaica, London, Schilthorn, Thailand, Whitby and Transylvania, it can now be concluded that the act of making tangible a piece of the imagination takes, in practice, two forms. One can discern a rational mode and an emotional-intuitive mode.

Rational Mode

The first mode concerns a rational search for the 'truth' behind a story. Many media tourists assert that they spend a considerable amount of time and attention in tracing the locations where a film, television series or novel has been played out, in order subsequently to make a detailed comparison in situ between the diegetic space of the stories and the physical-material space which they encounter at these locations. Concrete aspects are compared such as journey distances, the number of steps in a staircase, the size and dimensions of a building, the kinds of nature, the direction and flow of the traffic.

Although the rational mode recurs in all three cases, it comes to the fore particularly for fans of Bond and fans of the television detectives *Inspector Morse*, *Baantjer* and *Wallander*. Many Bond fans, for example, seem to make stills of important 'on location' scenes before they set off, so that they can subsequently take their own photograph from the same perspective, with the ultimate goal of investigating in detail and revealing the difference between 'reel' and 'real'. The fans of *Baantjer* exhibit similar behaviour. The author Appie Baantjer (who passed away in 2010), regularly received letters from readers, in which they illustrated in a friendly but resolute way the 'impossibility' of certain passages – in most cases related to the routes taken by detective De Cock.

What these fans are actually doing is internalizing and reliving the investigative activities of the films, series and books concerned. Just like their beloved detectives or superspies, these fans embark on an investigation in search of the truth, rooting around from clue to clue, and fussing over details in order to establish a difference between facts and false trails. The essence for them lies not so much in what they find as in the process of discovery. In other words, this involves a rational structure of detection and investigation, in which reality and imagination are brought face to face.

As comprehensively dealt with in Chapter 2, question marks can be placed against such a rigid contrast between reality and imagination. In practice, reality and imagination often complement each other quite appropriately. On the one hand, imagination is to a great extent based on the sensory experience of our physical surroundings; it is the creative reworking of what we are already familiar with. On the other hand, it is not possible to acquire an unequivocal picture of reality without using one's imagination to some degree. It is the power of the imagination which musters all our sensory stimuli together to the point where we experience 'the' reality. The imagination shuttles as it were, between idealistic concepts and sensory experience. In this sense, reality and imagination are not divorced from each other but interwoven and mutually dependent.

This, however, as was set out in the chapter concerned, is not to deny the fact that many people really have the need for a clear and fundamental separation between both of these qualities. And that is precisely what occurs in what we have called the 'rational mode'. By reflecting the world of the imagination in the physical characteristics at a location, sometimes in an almost geometric manner, the symbolic distinction between reality and imagination acquires a tangible and seemingly 'natural' character.

Emotional-intuitive Mode

The second mode concerns a more emotional, intuitive search for *bodily proximity*. Many of the media tourists interviewed derive no pleasure from a rational comparison between reality and imagination, but want to become themselves part of the world of the imagination and to experiance this 'alternative' world themselves. For this reason the detective fans wander through the streets of Oxford, Amsterdam and Ystad, past the houses and crime scenes of their beloved detective. They want to visit the bars where the detectives always hang out, so that they can sit on their stools and drink their drinks, be they cognac (Baantjer), a pint of beer (Morse) or a cup of coffee (Wallander). These fans want to get the feeling that their beloved detective could at any moment come walking round the corner, or just up the road – look, there! – might step out of the police station.

In a similar way, Dracula fans undertake the same journey as Jonathan Harker did around 100 years before. They stay in the same hotels and enjoy the same meals as Harker – 'robber steak' – served with a glass of blood wine. During the interviews Dracula fans tell of how exciting they find it to be in the land of Count Dracula themselves. They speak of the power of the attraction which the Count exerts on them and the erotic tension which his threatening presence generates – like a subliminal death wish. The story of Dracula is a story of sex, death and repressed desire – carnality steams from its pages. Of course, this has an influence on the make-up of the Dracula Tour. During the seven-day journey, locations from Dracula are combined with important places from the life of Vlad Dracula (a blood-thirsty, fifteenth-century prince, who according to some authors was the inspiration for the Dracula character) and other 'dark' locations such as torture chambers, prisons and graveyards. This immersion in stories about death and suffering make the Dracula Tour seem more like a trip into the underworld, in which the tourist, like a latter day Orpheus, becomes confronted with the vulnerability of the human body.

However, ultimately there are limits to the need for bodily proximity. In the case of the Dracula Tour there is certainly a sense of a voyage into the underworld, but at the same time, the journey takes place within the comfortable context of the 'tourist bubble'. The tourists experience a sense of Otherness, but always from a position of safety and cleanliness. Symptomatic of this are the plastic gloves, which are handed out to participants in the Baantjer Tour, before they take the fingerprints of a hired-in homeless person. Ultimately it is this thin plastic layer that keeps both worlds apart.

Even Bond fans, who generally take pride in the rational nature of their fascination (they prefer to talk about 'investigating the actuality' and 'finding out about the technical process of filming'), are sometimes in the grip of their own imaginations. Once on the spot, it overcomes almost every Bond fan: suddenly he finds himself standing with his legs slightly apart and his right hand in the air as if he were holding a gun. These Bond fans too talk about being 'engrossed' in the world of Bond: about how their physical presence at the correct locations, perhaps combined with adopting a certain pose or sometimes acting out complete scenes, induces in them the feeling that they have themselves become a part of a Bond adventure. They also tell of how it is to be caught up in the excitement and the 'thrill', which is so characteristic of the life of their beloved superspy.

Of course, the rational mode and the emotional-intuitive mode are not entirely separate from one another. It is after all possible to cross the line between imagination and reality after this symbolic boundary has been defined and marked out. In this sense, the rational mode is a logical instigator of the emotional-intuitive mode. Disenchantment is followed by re-enchantment. Sometimes each mode follows the other in the experience of an independent traveller. In other situations there is a larger travelling group, in which the internal group dynamic leads to a division of modes among the various group members. Regardless of comparable practical variations, in both cases a similar pattern emerges, and we should be able to identify an underlying dynamic of the imagination.

The Circuit of the Imagination

The concept of 'imagination' has been regarded with suspicion for a long time in Western thinking. Early Christians even thought that the imagination constituted a real danger, which lay at the heart of one of the worst sins – adultery. In the ages of Reason and Enlightenment, movements which exerted a dominant influence on Western philosophy, imagination was interpreted as the opposite of reason. It was considered a human weakness, an obstacle in mankind's progress towards self-fulfillment. Imagination was directly compared to loss of control (Huppauf and Wolf 2009).

Various thinkers have in later times tried to reassess the idea of imagination. Most notable among these is the Romantic school of the late eighteenth century, for whom the power of the imagination was a requirement for creativity and innovation. These thinkers ultimately acknowledged the same Kantian dichotomy between imagination and reason, but drew different conclusions as to their value; for them rationalism meant a simplification of human thinking while the creative power of the imagination on the other hand constituted the noblest good.

Notwithstanding similar efforts, the concept of 'imagination' still suffers a perverse reputation in the scientific world. It is at best regarded as a counterpart to reason and at worst as the domain of romantic, unscientific drivel. It still plays a minimal role even in the disciplines of media studies and cultural studies. And that is a shame, because it is in just this sort of discipline that it has an important contribution to make. Where accepted terms like 'representation' and 'text' place the emphasis on *conveyors of meaning* the concept of the imagination shifts the attention onto the underlying process of *interpretation of meaning*. Imagination offers the possibility to build a bridge between research domains which as a rule are studied separately from one another: the fields of production and consumption, for example; or the processes of individual interpretation of meaning and collective interpretation; or representations in media on the one hand and personal ideas and actions on the other.

This potential has not remained unnoticed. Recently various authors have argued the case for a re-evaluation and instrumentalization of the concept of imagination within the fields of media studies (Crouch, Jackson and Thompson 2005) and cultural philosophy (Huppauf and Wolf 2009). This book marches in step with these recent initiatives. In previous chapters, first a theory about imagination was set out, after which in subsequent chapters, the theory was adapted to the phenomenon of media tourism. The basis for this was the notion that imagination and reality are intrinsically connected with each other: things that are imagined emanate from sensory experience and conversely the power of the imagination is needed to channel the profusion of sensory stimuli into a clear notion of 'the' reality. Simultaneously, many people rightly feel the need to make a clear separation between these two concepts; imagination and reality are, as a rule, experienced as two distinct worlds. This paradoxical relationship leads, so it is supposed, to a circular process – the circuit of the imagination. In the case of media tourism, this can be split into four consecutive phases:

1. Physical places inspire artists;
2. Artists construct places that they have imagined;
3. Imagined places are appropriated by fans; and
4. Fans go in search of physical references to imagined places (see Figure 2.1 on page 17).

Our empirical research into the television detectives, James Bond and Dracula has given further substance to this theory and has generated a number of surprising results. For example, as became clear in the preceding chapters, stories do not just come out of the blue. The authors and filmmakers who were researched derived their inspiration to no small degree from their experience and knowledge of existing places. In the case of the detective tours, it seemed that all three original authors had personal experience of the locations in which their detectives were situated: Henning Mankell (author of *Wallander*) lived for some time on a farm just outside Ystad; Colin Dexter (author of *Morse*) still lives in Oxford and Appie Baantjer (author of *Inspector De Cock*, filmed under the title of *Baantjer*) worked for a long time in Amsterdam. Visiting the locations formed an important part of the writing process. Colin Dexter, for example, described during his interview how, before writing a Morse novel, he first did some research into the location: he wandered through the streets that he would later describe and talked to local residents on the street and in the pubs in order to get a taste of the *couleur locale*. In Appie Baantjer's case, one can even point to years of personal experience as a police detective in the Red Light District; an experience which, in his own words, leant considerable substance to the stories about Inspector De Cock.

Personal experience, however, is not actually necessary. Bram Stoker's description of Transylvania is very detailed and paints a vivid picture; thousands of people have been inspired by his words to relive the journey of Jonathan Harker. But strikingly enough, Stoker himself never actually set foot in Romania; he based his description entirely on literary travel stories and existing descriptions that he dug up in the National Library in London.

Nevertheless, we can see also from the case of *Dracula* how many stories are located somewhere. We may not be conscious of it, but almost every popular story – be it in the form of a novel, a film or a television series – is played out in a recognizable environment, to which can be ascribed a location. Stories become, so to speak, grafted onto existing landscapes (or cityscapes), a process through which symbols of local identity become exhibited and reproduced. Or, to reverse the reasoning, these stories contribute something to the *tourist gaze* of Oxford, Amsterdam, Ystad or Transylvania. They 'inject' the landscape with narrative meaning, giving it a meaning which delves below the surface of the image. Perhaps there are two genres which regularly deviate from this rule: *science fiction* and *fantasy*. It may, however, be regarded as typical that this is often the type of story in which undue attention is paid to the description of the 'ficticious' geographical environment (a striking example being the geofiction of *The Lord of the Rings*).

What the fieldwork also brought to the attention is how strongly making acquaintance with the physical landscape is directed by themes and viewpoints from the world of the imagination. For example, we found that the set-up and structure of the television detective tours owes a large debt to the characteristics of the content of the relevant television series. As far as narrative development is concerned, the tours offer an equivalent 'montage' of different locations, spread over the city and varied with short walks. At the centre lies the perspective of the detective, which, just as in the series, promises access to the darkest secrets of the local community. The tourist goes literally *backstage*, and is promised an apparently legitimate glimpse at the life and wounded body of another. Behold the universal attraction of crime stories and the underlying voyeuristic desire. With the detective as a surrogate, people can creep literally and figuratively under the skin of an unknown person.

In a similar sort of way, Bond tourism seems to be based on a synergy between espionage and tourism. Bond fans follow in the footsteps of their beloved spy, as they tell us in the interviews, and get access to locations from the novels and films, where denial of access seems to serve more as a recommendation than as a deterrent. The participants are, like Bond, predominantly white men in middle age, who enter and traverse the exotic landscape of the Other. These Bond tourists are different from 'normal' tourists because they have a mission: localizing, pinpointing and consuming the world of Fleming's imagination. The term 'Fleming effect' has in the past been used for Ian Fleming's trademark of ending every chapter with a *cliffhanger*. This effect can also be regarded as the desired state for any Bond tourist: to have the feeling of being absorbed into the adventurous *rush* of Bond – of being carried round in the maelstrom of his life.

Finally, what was also noticeable during the research was the way in which the physical reality was adapted to the imagined reality. In some cases small adaptations were made to street furniture. For example, various information boards were placed in the streets of Ystad, with which the association with *Wallander's* Ystad was physically acknowledged. In other cases names were changed. In Oxford a pub – as a result, among other factors, of pressure from competing initiatives – was renamed 'the' Inspector Morse Pub. In Amsterdam a café in the Jordaan neighbourhood that had partly been the model for the local pub of Inspector De Cock was rechristened '*Smalle Lowietje*', the name of the café in the series. In the mountains of Transylvania, an entire neogothic castle hotel, The Dracula Castle Hotel, was built more or less at the location where Bram Stoker's story was originally set.

Similar commercial initiatives notwithstanding, the municipalities of Amsterdam, Transylvania and Ystad also exhibited a certain reserve with respect to media tourism – certainly whenever the theme of the media product concerned did not coincide with the image desired by the local council or tourist office. Other organizations also sometimes had their doubts. At first police officers in Ystad were to say the least suspicious when asked on the street by tourists for a photograph or for information about *Wallander*. However, with the help of an enthusiastic press officer, attitudes were reversed and stories about *Wallander* became a common point of reference among police officers, for example in the use of nicknames for colleagues and in describing certain cases as being 'typically Wallander'. In this case, the imagination, itself a product of reality, was developed into an independent point of reference and frame of interpretation for one's own daily life.

Imagination and Memory

One last question remains, concerning the relationship between imagination and memory. As described in the previous chapter, the work of the French historian, Pierre Nora, has made an important contribution to this research. Nora's investigation into the working of the collective memory lay at the heart of the concept of places of the imagination, as developed in this book. But where Pierre Nora focused on collective memory, the focus of this book shifts to the collective imagination. How has this shift ultimately been manifested in practice?

What can first of all be concluded from the research is that *memoria* plays a significant role in the phenomenon of media tourism: memories of the past and the act of remembering itself crop up repeatedly in the cases researched and recur on different levels.

Firstly, many media tourists commemorate in situ the production process that lies at the heart of the imagined world. For example, Bond fans speak most respectfully of the EON team who produced the James Bond movies and they regard visiting the film locations as a mark of respect to the filmmakers. Once there, they try to get a clear picture of precisely how the films were recorded and what sort of physical problems or obstacles the film crew were confronted with. Although this aspect of things plays a lesser role with the other two parties researched, participants in the television detective tours and the Dracula Tour are regularly given details of the production process – normally in the form of 'amusing' anecdotes about the behaviour of the actors off stage or snippets of information about the camera techniques used.

Secondly, for many participants visiting places of the imagination sets in motion a process of reminiscence. By being on the spot themselves and calling to mind certain features of the story or even imitating them, not only do they make the story and the production process come to life, but they also trigger associated memories. What many media tourists for example speak about is the memory of making their first acquaintance with the story. Dracula fans think with pleasure back to the first time they read Stoker's novel or watched one of the film versions. The same goes for Bond fans. Most of them find all 22 films interesting but have a special connection with the Bond film that they saw for the first time in the cinema. They all speak lovingly of a recurring memory: how they as youngsters first entered the confined space of the cinema, mostly accompanied by their father to lose themselves for an hour and a half in the world of James Bond. These memories of their youth and of their father in their turn summon more general memories about this period of their lives. By visiting Bond locations and comparing the current landscape with what it looked like in the film, the Bond fans, as described in an earlier chapter, see what has been changed over the years – not only in themselves and in Bond, but also in the wider cultural landscape of which they both form a part.

Finally the dividing line between imagination and memory is often difficult to draw. The discussion about the historical background of Dracula is typical of this. According to research from the 1970s, the character Dracula can be traced back directly to the historical figure Vlad Tepes. Although strong doubts about this association have arisen among later literary historians, many tourists eagerly swallow it up. For them the historical authenticity of Vlad Tepes heightens the appeal of Dracula and vice versa: Vlad Tepes has been made interesting because of his association with Count Dracula. This two-way relationship also crops up during the Dracula Tour, in which visiting Dracula locations is combined with visiting the locations which have something to do with the life or death of Vlad Tepes. During the tour, it is true, the Romanian guides make considerable efforts to emphasize the separation of the fictitious and the historical, but in the experience of the tourists, the stories of blood-drinking vampires, burning people and impaling political opponents flow together into a single universe: the dark *place-myth* of Transylvania. We can identify a comparable process in the Baantjer Tour, in which stories about detective De Cock are freely intermingled with information about historical crimes that really took place, a combination which has resulted in the Red Light District in Amsterdam acquiring an ambiguous sort of crime folklore.

To resume, memory seems to play an important part in the way in which places of the imagination are experienced. In other words, one can identify a certain reciprocity between memory and imagination. Places like Transylvania and the Red Light District in Amsterdam derive their identity from a complex combination of memories and imagined events, from a system of stories in which events, whether fictitious or not, are placed side by side. These places are 'authentic' because they provide the decor for the stories – historical and fictional. Simultaneously, the stories are experienced as 'real' because they are put into place.

The concept of places of the imagination is – even more so than its forerunner *lieux de mémoire* – a good tool for charting this dynamic process. Where Nora took the historical authenticity of a location as his starting point, this book describes the reverse process: how people, starting with their imagination, go in search of physical, material references. They use the world to give shape to their ideas – in order literally to give a place to their fantasies, dreams and feelings of fear as well as solidarity. These ideas can have ties to the past. Seen from this perspective, memory is no more or less than the imagination of the past. Equally, there can also be ideas or stories about the present and the future. Even utopias and dystopias cry out for a *locus*.

Without imagination there remains little of the world as we know it. However, imagination alone is not enough. If we want to form a picture of our own past, present and future – our experience of being in the world – then our imaginations have to take on also a tangible form. It is precisely in this twilight zone between a realized imagination and an imagined reality that media tourists hope to find their answers.

Appendix

Some Notes on the Fieldwork

The goal of this book is to offer a truthful account of the research that I have conducted over the past few years. I have attempted to paint a clear picture of the research process: from the initial questions which lie at the heart of this project and the theoretical hypotheses to the final results of the research. Every chapter describes how the fieldwork was conducted and what questions I asked when confronted with the actuality.

However, things often get lost in the recording of a process like this. In the writing, the whole process becomes streamlined and tends to offer up the implicit suggestion that the whole project has gone smoothly and proceeded in a straight line towards its goal. Writing a book forces the researcher, as it were, to link questions and answers seemlessly to one another. In practice things are usually less polished. This research project into media tourism also encountered numerous diversions, doubts, adaptations over time and – in one particular case – an outright slip-up.

What I would like to do in this addendum is to make this raw reality, in a sense, more visible and to show what process preceded my conclusions. With that aim in mind, I have selected one interview per segment of research, which, in my opinion, is representative of the whole body of interviews or exemplifies it in the way in which it differs from the whole. Interviews are not the only kind of data collection used in this project – there are also observations and textual analysis – but the interviews can be regarded as the most important source and the most direct way of gaining access to the life world of the media tourist. The three interviews concerned are transcribed in the following paragraphs.[1] Each transcript is preceded by a short reflection.

Interview with Ewa-Gun

One of my first contacts in the field consisted of a six-day stay in Ystad, a small harbour town in the South of Sweden that enjoys some renown as the residence of the television detective Kurt Wallander. I stayed in a hotel in the centre of the town and tried, during the day, to interview as many tourists as possible, as well

---

1   In an attempt to make the transcripts more readable, the interviewees' repetitions and lapses in discourse have been, as far as possible, removed and the interviews shortened where necessary.

as local business people, civil servants and others involved. Beforehand, I had in my mind a clear separation between individual tourists on the one hand and organizations and interest groups on the other. Therefore I took it for granted that the former group would be mainly driven by personal, idealistic motives and the latter group, in a more calculating way would be trying to attain certain socio-political or commercial goals. I wanted to integrate both of these perspectives into my research.

Naturally the police station in Ystad stood high on my list of places to visit; after all this building features prominently in the books and films about Wallander. In line with the attitude mentioned in the last paragraph, I was particularly interested in the way in which the Ystad police reacted to the popularity of *Wallander* and to what extent they made use of the opportunity for free publicity.

During the interview with spokeswoman Ewa-Gun, it seemed that the Ystad police were indeed conscious of the publicity possibilities offered by *Wallander* tourism. The police were even actively involved in escorting the film crew and spoke highly of the 'Wallander effect' in terms of attitudes to officers on the street. At the same time, however, there seemed to be more to it than that. Ewa-Gun was in fact not only a spokeswoman for the police but at the same time a big fan of *Wallander*. She felt she could identify closely with the character Kurt Wallander precisely because he was a police officer and drew various parallels between the world described in the story and her own life as a police officer. This personal point of view brought to light how at the local police station, *Wallander* had grown into a much-used point of reference among police officers, for example in the making up of nicknames for colleagues and referring to specific crimes as 'Wallander cases'.

In other words, I realised from this interview that the separation that I had made in my own mind between the personal and the organizational was too simplistic, and that similar organizations should be regarded not only as faceless institutes (as parties with a specific socio-political agenda) but also as specific working environments, each with their own living culture. By keeping this in mind – the cultural habitat of organizations – I began to look for a broader and more refined perspective on the integration of media tourism into local communities.

Transcript: 01-B-04
Respondent: Ewa-Gun (55, police spokesman, Ystad, Sweden)
Location: Ystad (Sweden), July 12, 2007

Interviewer: First of all thanks for your cooperation. Let me introduce you to the purpose of the research. As I told you before, I am working on a research project that focuses on media tourism: the phenomenon of people visiting locations that are related to famous novels, films or TV serials. The research results will be published maybe next summer or next year in an article and a book based on *Inspector*

Morse, Baantjer and *Wallander*. And another case: *The Da Vinci Code*. To start with, how do you feel about *Wallander*?

Respondent: He's one of my best friends actually.

Interviewer: OK. Why is he one of your best friends?

Respondent: Because, when I came here – it's five years ago in September – I came from Stockholm. I have worked at the police academy there as their public information officer. This is a small town. So when I came here they wondered what is she going to do. I felt lonely and then I could see: Wallander was here. I have read all the books and I have been helping out when they did the first movie. Wallander was nearby me and when I came to Ystad I felt he was here sometimes. He was a good friend. And then when they started up the production of this movies. They asked me as a public information officer, it's in my role, to help them to create the police station, the manuscript and the new actor. I became also a friend. You hang out. I prefer my fantasy version of it.

Interviewer: The novel?

Respondent: As a police officer he is a human being. He thinks a lot of the situation nearby him, but also in the world. He's sad person. He has been married and it's been a failure. We are just similar. I had also had a divorce. The guilt you feel to your children. And I had to raise them up. I have worked so much and sometimes I haven't been there for my daughters. We talked a lot about it today and that's why I think there is a difference between me and Kurt. I'm a woman. I can easier share my feelings and cry, but I can also feel the sorrow in the hearts. When it's too much for me I grab a bottle of wine or glass of whisky and listen to opera. It's a big feeling. You can scream easier with a glass of wine. I've seen it all. I've been a police officer for 35 years now. I've seen human beings behave like bastards. I've seen police colleagues behave very badly. I've seen fantastic police work from many police officers nearby me. Kurt has a lot of feelings that I like about him. He thinks about things. Sometimes I don't do the way he does things. Because he is rushing away and has his gun in his pocket or in his desk in his office and that's totally forbidden. He is a little bit a one-mans-performance. Police work is always a performance in group. There is a big difference. Otherwise there isn't a good story.

Interviewer: You mentioned that you cooperated with the studio for the last movies. Why did you choose to cooperate with the studio?

Respondent: First of all it's in my role as a public information officer to take care of these assessments. But if I had felt it wasn't in my heart, I had said no. It's a little bit of a performance for me as well. I like culture, music and films, so therefore it's good.

Interviewer: You like Kurt Wallander.

Respondent: Ooh yes. I do.

Interviewer: So there are personal motives. But I guess there were also other motives – some sort of strategy from the press office of the police to whether or not cooperate with the film producers?

Respondent: We had to ask the county commissioner. They said you had to make it clear that we must do our normal work first of all and then you can … But I've been a police officer for so many years now, so I have a professional way of doing things. And I had my holiday that year when we did the first movie. So I was there every day in my vacation. I was there from 8 in the morning till the end of the day. It was important for me to have a good quality in the dialogues and in the scenes. It was the first movie and the director of the movie – he was a great director from Stockholm. We got on very well together. He asked me; I was there all the time. We taught him how to behave with a gun. We taught him how to walk and talk as a police officer. I asked a very young police woman, she was new here in Ystad: could you please help Johanna to be a good young police woman? They got on very well together. So it was very good. We had very good dialogues and then the actor created his role. It was Krister Henriksson's first *Wallander* movie. He was sitting here in our cafeteria and he was looking at us. How do they do it? What are they saying? And because he's a very good actor he could take it in and then repeat it. It was actually an amazing experience for me. And then when they did the other films I was there to answer questions at the Internet and I was on the place when they did the filming. I always helped them when they were filming in the traffic. I was there as a police officer to secure that something didn't happen to them.

Interviewer: Do you think that the *Wallander* novels and movies have influenced the image of the police?

Respondent: Yes absolutely. Especially the first film and then the police force… There were so many people interested in us. We felt a little bit proud. That was a very important thing, because in Sweden there is some proudness forgotten. We are too much like: I'm sorry that I'm a police officer. I think we should be proud of ourselves, because if we are proud we do a better work. And then there were many tourists. They would stop the patrol cars down in Ystad. Can we take photos of you? We are from Germany, we are from England. First they were a little bit embarrassed, but now I've asked them if you can do it. It is public relations. I think it's good for the police force of Ystad to have Wallander.

Interviewer: You noticed some were a little bit embarrassed at first.

Respondent: No, not embarrassed, but shy.

Interviewer: How do you notice they are more proud of their work because of Wallander?

Respondent: Because Wallander is strong. The books are very spread around all of the world and the interest for the police station and Kurt Wallander's office has been huge. We have had many visitors. For each visit here they have accepted Kurt as a colleague. Sometimes when I walk around with groups I will ask to a colleague: 'Hello Jan, have you seen Kurt today?' They will say: 'He doesn't work here'. But there are also colleagues who will say to me: 'Ooh shit, you missed him, he just went out the door'. Then you can see the visitors …

Interviewer: What kind of visitor are those?

Respondent: Journalists of course who are making a report about it. But there are also tourists and there are some from Norway.

Interviewer: So tourists come to the office?

Respondent: They come like you. If I'm in the house they call me. If I'm here and I'm on duty and I have time for it. I always will say sorry I can't deal with this today or I have a couple of minutes, let's take a look at Kurt Wallander's office. He isn't in today, but you never know.

Interviewer: When I came in this morning you also made a joke with the person at the desk.

Respondent: The first time I realized the importance of Kurt Wallander here. When I was here 14 days I didn't liked it here and when I was down at the reception she was here and there was a tourist like you. She said: 'Kurt Wallander doesn't exist, it is just a book'. I said: 'What did you say? Absolutely he does'. I did it like this. I called the woman Ebba. And after a while she liked it. After a week or two she accepted it and I also noticed that the other ladies in the reception are looking a little bit with envy at her.

Interviewer: You only call her Ebba when the tourists are here?

Respondent: No, I think it is important to her. I say to her: you *are* her.

Interviewer: And are there more examples of this?

Respondent: We had a visit from Sweden, from the Swedish film institute. I think it was the beginning of this year. Everyone was a film worker. They all worked with films in one or another way. And I was standing in the lobby down there and an elderly colleague came by. I said: 'Didn't you notice? It was Kurt'. Everyone looked, was it, was it? Everyone was so totally... After ten seconds they all realized and we laughed for three to four minutes. I had a visit from the USA and they came to Sweden one year and then the Swedish family goes to America for one year and they do a change like this. Three years ago the American family visited Sweden and they wanted to visit Kurt Wallander's office. The Swedish family said it isn't possible. You know Kurt Wallander is a book. Yeah, but there's a place called Ystad. You know they had visited Internet. Somehow they heard about me and they phoned me. We are not crazy. We have this visit from the USA and is it possible to visit the Kurt Wallander office. I said: 'Of course it is'. They said: 'Another one who is crazy'. So I invited them here. This little man from America came in with a book in his hand. This is absolutely amazing. He was almost crying. I don't like this police station very much, it is ugly from the 1970s. He was so happy and he was standing and looking at the water tower. 'Ooh yeah, I've read about this'. He was so happy. And one morning I had a very early visit from a sailor from Germany. He arrived at Ystad and asked for a visit at the police station. I drove in to the station and I was telling them about the station. Suddenly some of the man said: 'There is something more here. I counted the steps from point A to B. There is 124 in the book, there is 122'. Some of the readers they really nail everything in the book.

Interviewer: Why do you think people who read crime fiction want to visit places from this fictional world?

Respondent: I think from the beginning Mr Kurt Wallander interested us because someone wrote about our area. You know Henning has a farm outside Ystad. He bought for 25 years ago. Mankell is a thinking person. He analyzes and he thinks. He makes stories of what he sees and what he thinks. Then he became… There is often fog here and he took his walks at the countryside. He began to find out this police officer from Ystad. Then the thoughts became the first book, the faceless killer, which I love. It's the best. It's my first contact with Kurt. And then he wrote about our area. When I read the book the first time I don't remember the crimes in it. I was only focused on the streets, the places. I knew every detail of the places. And then Kurt Wallander: he is an interesting person. So I think it has two points here: interesting dialogue and interesting story and then the person. He isn't a hero.

Interviewer: But if you're not from here – like the tourists from Germany – why do they want to come here and visit this location?

Respondent: I think it's because … It's the same phenomenon like Morse in England. And one of my daughters lives in England. I'm a little bit interested in how they're doing things. I'm very fond of Foyle. My absolute favorite is Peter Boyd, from *Waking the Dead*. They are planning a British version of *Wallander* next year. I pray every night: let it be Peter Boyd. He has this melancholy in the eyes. You must have the experience of life. You must have … My daughter loves him and sends over the DVDs. I can see his sorrow. Not with Barnaby. He has an ordinary family live. It makes you feel safe. I have a hectic live myself, because my daughter is going to marry this English man, my future son in law in 14 days. It's very difficult logistic. She's phoning every day, screaming and screaming. I'm very proud of England in a way. I don't know why.

Interviewer: Maybe because of this strong relation between England and the detectives genre?

Respondent: Yeah, something to do with detectives. Yes. I must have an English version of whatever. Tuesday nights we have Barnaby now…

Interviewer: Most questions have been raised. But just one question I still wanted to ask: you've got this funny thing with the reception – this character role. Do you notice other colleagues sometimes making similar jokes about it, so to say in the more general office culture here at Ystad Police?

Respondent: Sometimes when we have a new crime coming up. We have had several heavy crimes here the last years. Someone tried to drive a car right in the coffee room five o'clock one morning. It was heavy. In the beginning a touch of crime we could say if this was a Wallander novel. We had a pyromaniac three years ago. In one night he put on six buildings in fire in one and a half hours. We felt wow this like in a Kurt Wallander movie. Sometimes, now we have the movie. Next year there will be a new movie, with a new crew and they will ask for police newspapers, some uniforms and now. They always ask on the last minute.

Interviewer: To conclude. You have this personal affection with Kurt Wallander and on the other hand it's very positive for the image of the police and you noticed especially among the police men themselves.

Respondent: Some of them. Those who have open minds.

Interviewer: Do you also notice something new among the people living in Ystad?

Respondent: Yes, especially to me. I'm called the very special Kurt Wallander police. You know I think this a very nice. You know there are many newspapers about it. I've tried to save them for my children. Here, let me show you.

Interviewer: Wonderful. And thanks a lot for the interview.

Interview with Gunnar

Interviews conducted over the telephone are far from ideal. One misses non-verbal modes of communication and the physical distance between interviewer and respondent makes it difficult to establish a bond of trust. However, in some cases there is no other option. In the section of research into James Bond, it was simply impossible to interview all the respondents face-to-face because the fans and locations were spread so far apart. Therefore, the interviews with Bond fans were conducted by and large over the telephone.

One of the exceptions to this was the interview with Gunnar. This Swedish respondent turned out in fact to be not only a Bond fan and Bond traveller, but was also the proprietor of an actual Bond museum. Outside of his work as a dealer in car parts, he had set up a space with countless pieces of Bond memorabilia, film posters and merchandising, where for a small entrance fee, visitors could wander round. That in itself was sufficient reason for me to make an exception and travel personally to Nybro so that I could interview Gunnar within the very walls of his own museum.

The interview with Gunnar contained other reasons for making it a special case. As the existence of the Bond musuem led one to suspect, Gunnar was more than just an average fan. He was not only interested in the films and books but also identified strongly with the underlying life stories of James Bond and his creator Ian Fleming. It was particularly poignant to hear Gunnar's story of the mysterious disappearance of his father, especially in relation to his adoration for the Bond/Fleming duo. Although Gunnar differed from the average Bond fan in terms of emotional involvement, this interview showed how important popular culture (and visiting the places associated with it) can be in people's everyday life.

Transcript: 02-A-11
Respondent: Gunnar (57, car parts salesman and director of James Bond Museum, Kalmar, Sweden)
Location: Nybro (Sweden), September 13, 2008

Interviewer: As I mentioned in my e-mail, I have some questions about James Bond: about the fan culture, about your James Bond museum, and especially about your journeys related to James Bond. I'm interviewing around 20 James Bond fans and I'm using all the interview data to write an academic paper and book about the whole topic. If I'm going to cite you, I will use your full name, if that's no problem.

Respondent: That's okay.

Interviewer: First … your name is Gunnar, yes?

Respondent: The real name is Nils Gunnar Bond James.

Interviewer: Okay, yes. You added James Bond to your real name? You also went to the city council? To sort of officially …

Respondent: Yeah. To the Swedish government. And they accepted it. So I have Bond, James on my license driving.
Interviewer: Nice, yeah.

Respondent: Just one year ago, they agreed with that.

Interviewer: Yeah. And why did you ask for that? Why did you ask …

Respondent: Uhm ... I want to celebrate Ian Fleming. I want to celebrate my father who disappeared in 1959.

Interviewer: Hmhm.

Respondent: And I also want to connect all these things, like my house in Kalmar, I called it Golden Eye.

Interviewer: Okay.

Respondent: This estate I have in Kalmar. Because I want to celebrate in honor to Ian Fleming. So I also want to take in the name Bond, my name is Bond, James Bond, to add to the complete idea about the museum, my house and Bond and all like that. That's the reason that I want to have the name also. Bond, James Bond.

Interviewer: Yeah. And you told me that you also want to honor your father. He disappeared in 1959?

Respondent: I don't know if you know about my father? During the Second World War, he was fighting for Germany against England. And after that he came to Sweden in 1945 and got married to my mother in 1950. Uh, so I have two brothers also. So one day he decided to go back to Germany on a holiday in 1959.

Interviewer: Yeah.

Respondent: And after that we've never seen him.

Interviewer: Okay.

Respondent: Perhaps he could be in shock or he could have been disappeared ... It's ... It's a mystery.

Interviewer: Strange, yes

Respondent: ... It's a strange mystery. So that's the one reason for turning Fleming into my stepfather, as consent ...

Interviewer: Okay, yes. Yeah.

Respondent: So I have someone, to rely on and someone that can learn me things or how to do things in my way. Perhaps I compare Ian Fleming and my father to each other in my dreams. Ian Fleming and my father have the same, the same uh, experience during the second war, but for different countries.

Interviewer: Of course. Yes, yes. England versus Germany.

Respondent: But the situations in the self it's the same, in the mind and in the brain. They are only different countries.

Interviewer: Fighting for their own country.

Respondent: Yeah, yeah. Exactly. So, when I grew up my, my thinking about my father was stronger and stronger. So I tried to do research about where he could have gone and I didn't find any answers. So that's the reason I took on Ian Fleming and after that I read a book, such novels, and when I became older I thought: Perhaps I could do some collecting of Bond movies and posters and cars and all like that. After a while I thought: Why don't you have an exhibition in the library in Nybro and I did that. And after that I collected more. And finally I made an exhibition in cinema Kalmar.

Interviewer: Yeah, yeah.

Respondent: And after that I thought: Why not take the next step. So perhaps I can make some museum, because they don't exist in the world, no real, just for ... So that's to make a long story short. So that's the reason why I started the museum, why I took the name Bond James and why I called my house in Kalmar Golden Eye. That's where I'm living in.

Interviewer: Yeah. So you did sort of create this atmosphere. I mean, your own house is also in the James Bond style?

Respondent: I like the English style. It's different. It's my inspiration. In the toilet and bathroom I have soaps and perfumes and sheets and all like that. Just like Bond.

Interviewer: Fleming also lost his father when he was young, didn't he?

Respondent: Yeah. I think it's tragic for his family. So, I think there any many ways of thinking about how he lived and how he died. And other things, like the suicide of his son and the death of his wife.

Interviewer: Yes, but let's turn to a more practical question. How did you start the James Bond museum?

Respondent: I had a car parts store, so I did a little corner here and put something on the walls there … It was about perhaps 20 square meters.

Interviewer: Yes, so it started as part of a car repair building first, or a car sell shop? And then you turned it into a minor exhibition?

Respondent: It took a very long time before the idea came to the real.

Interviewer: And to make the collection of course.

Respondent: Yes, because if you do it like this, you have to work on it for about 15 to 20 years. It takes a long time to do this. You have to put in your money that you earn every week and every month.

Interviewer: Yeah.

Respondent: And you buy something and then you buy some more. And it takes … 15, perhaps 20 years to create something like this.

Interviewer: How many visitors do you get each year?

Respondent: I think about two, three thousand. It's a very little town here, you know. It takes a while to get here. We're living in the north and it's very cold in the winter, you know. It's not easy for people to come here.

Interviewer: And those two or three thousand visitors, what sort of, what sort of type of visitors is coming here to the museum? How would you characterize them?

Respondent: Well, for example, you've got a child like four, five years old. Perhaps he saw one Bond movie and was very enthusiast about Bond and like that. So he comes here with his family and pretends to be 007 himself

Interviewer: Yeah.

Respondent: … As we also do at this age. But you've also got girls coming here. You have many. I know a woman who was a neighbor to Sean Connery when he was 2 years old.

Interviewer: Hmm.

Respondent: So she went here four … four years ago and had some photo's when Sean Connery was just one or two years old. So she had … I think she was 75 or 76. So we have very different ages.

Interviewer: Yeah.

Respondent: And there are these girls who have travel one hundred thousand kilometer just to visit the museum.

Interviewer: Okay.

Respondent: She and her sister and her mum and dad came here and she was 15 years old and her sister was 17.

Interviewer: Yeah.

Respondent: And she adored Maud Adams, like that. She wants to look like her. And she got around for several hours; just to have a look, feel the inspiration and smell, feel, like that.

Interviewer: Yeah.

Respondent: Yeah, yeah. And many people also from school come here.

Interviewer: And what do you want visitors to experience or what's the main goal of your exhibition?

Respondent: The main reason to have the visitors here and the main reason they want to come is that everyone has a connection with Bond and with the real places related to Bond. I mean, you have got a lot of these places to visit all over the world. And I think you recognize yourself in the Bond movies and they have made some mark for a long time and everybody knows a thing about 007 or James Bond in a way. So when I started to do research in 1956 ... I tried to go a museum myself. A Bond museum, because I am very interested in Bond. So I travel around the world to look for a see Bond museum, but to my disappointment I find out there isn't any museum.

Interviewer: No.

Respondent: So why not do anything about that? Perhaps many people think the same like me. I want to travel around and see a Bond museum, because the last Bond movie was real, real good. So I want to, to explore a little more on my own experience. Not just looking at the films, but being inside some special place. Perhaps to be inside.

Interviewer: So you want to... You say that you want to give an experience not only watching the movies, but also go a little bit further, to be sort of inside world 007?

Respondent: Yeah.

Interviewer: Could you explain a little bit more about that sort of experience?

Respondent: Of course you're trying to recognize yourself in the many places from the Bond movies. You can also realize that in your real life.

Interviewer: But what does it ... I mean, if you wear a suit like Bond or you wear some other Bond-product, what gives it this special flavor?

Respondent: It depends on who you are and what you are thinking in relationship within yourself and the people who make the Bond character. Perhaps you like some specific Bond character, like Sean Connery, Timothy Dalton or Pierce Brosnan or perhaps you would be like him yourself and you've got this feeling. It's not so ...

Interviewer: I'm trying to analyze what makes it special. This atmosphere. Does it make life more exciting of does it offer more excitement, for instance? Or give more style or more uh ...

Respondent: I think you go in the footsteps, like Bonds' and Ian Flemings' ... I think you have to think about how Ian Fleming described the way he thought and the way he, perhaps his experience from the Second and the First World War. He had experiences as a journalist when he got to Italy. And he describes places in the book and Broccoli and Saltzman made some movies about that, they take place in different world cities. And then you go to the alley, you got to the place, the hotel and you get some feeling. Inside your brain you have an experience that you not can buy for money or anything. You have just gone there to get that right feeling for that moment.

Interviewer: Yeah.

Respondent: Then you go home again. Then you watch the movie the scene was in and then you recognize it: I've been there.

Interviewer: Yeah.

Respondent: And I think it's in your heart and in your brain you feel you have something in common with the movie and with the people and places in the movie. I think it's like an experience that you take to your heart and the brain. And you will be filled up with some universal feeling and all the feelings that you never can get in any other way.

Interviewer: Yeah.

Respondent: Yes, I'm thinking about today's situation: the global incidents. So you have a war today in all different places, different types of wars. You have problems in your safety. Perhaps you have problems in your family. You see, every part of the world is a problem, maybe not always, but you cannot deny it all because of the news, the newspapers, the television, they talk about it every day.

Interviewer: Yes.

Respondent: You have to fly away sometimes, because you ... You can't take it in your brain with all that, all the problems and shootings. You have to fly away and dream a little also. Because otherwise, it's all information from the bad side. You have to take in some good sides also.

Interviewer: Yeah. But the funny thing is that in this case the fictional world is also about violent shootings and about war and about terrorism and anti-terrorism.

Respondent: Yeah. Yes, that's right. But then you have the vile guy and you have the good guys in these movies. And the bad guy looses.

Interviewer: Yes.

Respondent: So you have an end. When the movie is over you have the problem solved.

Interviewer: Yeah. And there's a clear vision between right and wrong. Between the enemy and the hero, yeah.

Respondent: Yeah, exactly.

Interviewer: Well, let's go on to the next topic: Bond tourism. Because you visited Bond locations in Hamburg recently, didn't you? You visited the hotel, other parts of the James Bond movie. And what other locations have you visited?

Respondent: Uhm, of course I have been to Pinewood Studio and all the vacation places from Bond, and I have met a lot of people: Jaws, Richard

Kiel, and Guy Hamilton, Julias Goldman, many people who have made the Bond movies in the old times. Two days ago I visited hotel Atlantic Kempinski. There they made *Tomorrow Never Dies* in the scene that Pierce Brosnan and Teri Hatcher were having a conversation and were also having some sex, of course [laughs].

Interviewer: [laughs] Yes.

Respondent: Not unusual in Bond movies.

Interviewer: No.

Respondent: And ... So that's the way I think about my tours and my visits to places related to Bond. Or to visit sponsors who have been in the Bond movies ...

Interviewer: Yeah.

Respondent: I went to France, outside Reigns and also in France I, I go to a place call Oi or Oju or something.

Interviewer: Hmm.

Respondent: And there is Champagne house Bollinger. Yeah. It has been in the Bond movies for many years.

Interviewer: Yeah.

Respondent: And they have an agreement between the Broccoli family and the president who founded the Bollinger. So the champagne people told me: I don't have to say this, and maybe I shouldn't, but we don't pay anything to be in the Bond movies (laughs). Don't tell anyone! Don't tell anyone, because I have to kill you after that.

Interviewer: Yeah. Yeah.

Respondent: So you have a really hidden world out there. But we have also, we're sitting here, now in the museum and we call it Ice Palace. This palace here is built like a, Gustav Graves palace in *Die Another Day*. Because you have the walls, it's like ice. I took the inspiration because I wanted to have the walls white and the roof here, it's the same plastic as they used in *Die Another Day*.

Interviewer: Okay.

Respondent: This plastic here, they had 40 tons delivered to the Pinewood Studio at the time.

Interviewer: Yes. But back to the theme of tourism: You mentioned that you visited different sponsors like Bollinger.

Respondent: Yes.

Interviewer: And you visited this hotel in Hamburg. Did you visit other locations from the world of 007? You mentioned Venice, for instance.

Respondent: Yes. Venice. I went to Venice one year ago. And of course I went to the palace, the Hampton tower. And also to London. And as I said: I went to Pinewood Studio many, many times …

Interviewer: What do you do there? Because you mentioned that you went to the hotel in Hamburg. Did you also take pictures of yourself standing on top of the roof of the hotel?

Respondent: Of course. And I toke some pictures to put on the website. Because I want to have some shoots from the real film and some shoots of the visit when I was there, to show the people that everyone can do the same.

Interviewer: Uhu.

Respondent: Yeah. You know, anyone can do the same. If you want, you can go around the world in the footsteps of Bond and see all these places. And if I can do it, why don't you? I think it's the inspiration to give to anyone to go around and see places.

Interviewer: Yeah.

Respondent: But I think it's still interesting because sometimes you have seen it in Bond movies and you have not read any article about it after that. But you can't visit all places, because sometimes, for example, you have these special places where you have to go with the elevator up and you got to have these special keys. You got to have special permission to go there.

Interviewer: Yes. Well, Bond went there, right? But how does it … It's a difficult question, but how does it feel to sort of walk through the world of 007?

Respondent: Well, you can find peace inside yourself when you go round and see places like this.

Interviewer: Yes.

Respondent: I think it's something you … You get a special experience. So you have new angles to think about something. Perhaps you could be inside the films. You can also recognize it, as I said before. When you go home, you can see it again. And you get inside the feelings that you have been traveling all over the world and you are back in your hometown again and you can see it in your living room. And the world is not so big. Because you can travel over the world now.

Interviewer: Yeah.

Respondent: And you have this little experience now. I think it's great. You like uh … You get more feelings. You grow as a person I think, if you want to. It depends on what's the reason for doing it. I am a fan of Bond, the movies and everything like that. I think in my way, every people thinks in their own way and at the end nothing is wrong. Everyone can think about how it is to visit these places.

Interviewer: Yes. Well, most of my questions have been answered. Or is there something we didn't talk about, something that we should have discussed?

Respondent: Uhm. No, not for the moment.

Interviewer: Ok, thanks a lot.

Interview with Jonas

For the area of research concerning Dracula tourism I conducted a one-week long period of participatory observation with a group of American Dracula fans, who were travelling in a bus through Transylvania. The tour journeyed through scores of locations which had a connection with the ficticious count or with the life story of the historical figure Vlad Dracula. The intervening hours in the bus were spent watching vampire movies or other films from the horror genre. The interviews also took place in the bus. It was occasionally difficult to find a quiet place in the bus, a bit removed from the other travellers. However, the context of the bus trip also had a positive effect on the outcome of the interviews: it seemed as if the passing Romanian landscape stimulated the thought process and encouraged the respondents in their reflections.

Furthermore, the fact that I was part of the group for a week clearly added to the quality of this section of the research. Naturally, conversations with the Dracula fans were not limited to formal interviews during the bus trips; many informal discussions were held during the long evenings in the Dracula Castle Hotel in Brasov and in The Golden Crown Hotel. In this regard there was a clear contrast with the research into the James Bond fans, with whom little or no basis of trust could be created.

An example is the interview with Jonas. This American teacher from Chicago was in all facets an ideal respondent. He managed easily to find the words to express his visions and thoughts but also had no problem in articulating his emotions and intuitions. So the interview became not only a succession of questions and answers but a genuine conversation in which both interviewer and respondent were able to develop their ideas.

Looking at the transcript, it is noticeable how representative this interview is. Many of the feelings and ideas which Jonas expresses recur with the other respondents, not only among Jonas's fellow-travellers but also among the respondents from the other two segments of the research: the James Bond fans and the participants in television detective tours. Just like Jonas, these respondents spoke of the mysteries of the landscape, of identifying with the characters and of the tension between wanting to make a cognitive contrast between reality and imagination and the emotional desire to make both worlds come together.

Transcript: 03-A-07
Respondent: Jonas (33, teacher, Chicago, USA)
Loication: Transylvania, Romania, July 14 2009

Interviewer: First of all, thanks for cooperating with this research project. My questions will be going in different directions. Some are about the text itself: the novel and the movies. But I'm also interested in the tour, and more in general your experience of these landscapes … Just to start with, could you give me your name, age, place of residence and occupation?

Respondent: Jonas. I am 33. I live in Chicago, Illinois and I am a teacher, an elementary school teacher.

Interviewer: Well to start with the story itself: What attracts you in the story of Dracula?

Respondent: Well as far as the story goes: I watched the movies first. I grew up watching the black and white universal movies and then I read the book in seventh grade. What I really enjoyed about the story was that it was definitely different from any movie version I had seen. And every movie version even though they claim they stick to the book, they really don't. The book is unique onto itself. And what I love about the story is it's very classical. And every time I have read it – I've read it about three times now – I pull out something new. The way that Bram Stocker wrote it, it's just dripping with, you know, allegory and with ... well without going into the deep literature, it's ... you can break it down in so many aspects and you can talk about the, you know, Victorian London of that time versus ancient times. You can talk about it as kind of a fear of foreigners of that time. You can talk about it as a religious aspect, a sexual aspect, how Dracula and the blood, everything very akin to Christianity. You can ... you know the sexual aspects. You can break it down and study it in any number of ways. And I think that's why after a hundred of years, the book has never been out of print, because you can find so many things in it. So as a literary aspect, I enjoy that. As a story it's a great story of escape and menace and overcoming that menace.

Interviewer: And it's also got a lot different dimensions that sort of press the reader to find out more about it, right?

Respondent: Absolutely. That's one thing I am impressed with and continue to be impressed with: his description of everything, especially Bram Stocker's description of Transylvania because from my understanding he had never been to Transylvania. It was only through his studies in the libraries of London and that to me, his descriptions ... Today we are going through the Borgo Pass. Very excited to do that because of his descriptions and how he describes it you know, the land beyond the forests. So I wanted to see it with my own eyes and to really experience it. This is my way to kind of be Jonathan Harker. Be the character and go through the land as a stranger for the first time. Hopefully there's not a giant menace waiting for me, but ...

Interviewer: You talked about a 'real' experience? Could you elaborate more on that?

Respondent: Well, I'm lucky: I can watch a movie and really get into it. Feel very much for the characters. If I read a book I can, you know, the characters seem like my friends by the end of the book. I am able to be very emotionally involved with it. And so to me the next logical step is, you know, after I read something or watch a movie then I like to create things on my own. I make little video camera movies.

Interviewer: Oh yeah?

Respondent: Yeah. I've done it with live action, friends and family. But, also I do it with little figures, little monster toys I have. And I'll paint the background and build up little sets. And just little fun things for me to do, because then … I get inspired after I see something or I read something. It inspires me. I think that's fantastic and I don't want it to end and I put my own spin on it. And see what I can create. And like I said the natural extension is to come to the actual place and as far as, you know, loving the monster movies, well there's Egypt, which I love to go to, to visit the pyramids and the mummies. And you know, I've kind of been to Germany for Frankenstein. Even though the book takes place in Switzerland. But I don't think … Transylvania is so entrenched in Dracula. And it's interesting because this tour is a lot about Vlad Tepes, the person, which had nothing to do with the vampire. But, I think that that's how closely it's tied together. When you think of Dracula, you think of Transylvania almost at the same breathe. And because it's such a foreign and exotic land that not a lot of people go to. I don't know anyone who has been to Transylvania before or talked about it. But, to me it's such a natural. You know? To go there, to experience it and to see it, to breathe it and to taste it, in a way you can't on the pages of a book or on the pictures on a screen. For me I am just the kind of person, I wanted more. I didn't want to watch it on a two-dimensional screen or read it in black and white. I wanted to drink it all in.

Interviewer: [laughing] Yeah. And *eat* it all in, like the dinner that Jonathan Harker had.

Respondent: The robber steak. Although being a vegetarian I just had to watch other people eat the steak. But, then yeah. I like that little touch and that turn me on this particular tour was the little nuances, the way that they took aspects of the novel and really wanted to add those little things. You know, that attracted me greatly to that. And I really liked that little detail that really just … Any little thing to recreate such as beloved character.

Interviewer: Could you give an example of that?

Respondent: Well the robber steak, the dinner, recreating his one meal and Bram Stocker describes several different meals in the novel. Today going through the Borgo Pass, a nice little touch that they there elaborate on. Because we could have gone like a number of routes, but I like the fact that they specifically mention it that we're going to … You know, it's being pointed out as, 'Hey this is a part of the novel'. It's a tiny little part, but it's for fans of the novel that's …

Interviewer: For me that was one of the most interesting things to read, actually.

Respondent: I agree. Absolutely. Crossing the tracks. Going from the known to the unknown. Going to the first question that's another aspect that I enjoy too about the novel and I imagine even more so in 1897. The description he makes of Transylvania, that must have been very new to people. Probably they had no idea what it was like. And of course people didn't really travel, not nearly as much as they do now. So that would be their way of going there. So and this is a hundred years later, as I said, how many people have gone to Transylvania? That to me is kind of indicative. I want to do it then. People travel all around the world and oh there's a place that not a lot of people have gone to and it happens to be some place that I've always wanted to go to. That's just … It sparked it even more. Because when I told people that I am going to Transylvania, they'll kind of turn their heads and go, 'What! Really?'

Interviewer: It's like a land that doesn't exist, heh?

Respondent: Yeah! It almost seems like a fairytale land. Some kind, you know, something out of movie imagination, but it's not, it's a very real place.

Interviewer: Earlier we talked about the re-creative aspects. Could you elaborate on those aspects?

Respondent: It's an extension of enjoying, you know, you can read the book and you can enjoy the novel and then … But instead of putting the book down, you know, this whole tour is kind of becoming a character in the novel. And you get to … Well the beginning of the whole novel is Jonathan Harker's traveling. Well, that's exactly what we are doing. We're traveling. Because even getting on the plane and coming here you are traveling … And once you land in Transylvania and we're going through you really do feel like a character in the story. Specifically Jonathan Harker. And you get to see things for the first time, you get to taste foods for the first time, and you look at the Carpathian Mountains and how impressive they are for the first time, and that's all from the book. And that's literally; I am literally Jonathan Harker on this tour. And that is something that I enjoy. And that's probably this is more for the die-hard fan because not everybody … You can enjoy a book and you can enjoy a movie, but then that's it. You turn the TV off and you go do something else. But, for someone like me a little die-hard I want more, I need more. And this is just the ultimate … Unless there were real vampires running around, this is about the closest I can get to actually living out one of, if not my favorite story, my favorite book.

Interviewer: Living out the story, that's what it is about?

Respondent: Yeah. It is, you know.

Interviewer: But, what makes it so special?

Respondent: Because you get to experience it for yourself. Like I said, I'm lucky because I am able to emotionally invest myself into characters and events in a book. You know? [laughing] I remember one time I read a book and it was so sad and like I was bummed out for the rest of the day, because I was so upset with what was happening with the characters. So I'm really able to get into a book. And what makes it special is because I don't want to put a book down and walk away and do something else. I want to experience it as much as I can. And instead of just seeing, using my eyes and my ears, you know when I watch a movie … I want to taste it all in. I want to smell it and not just to look at a small TV screen and see a magnificent forest. I want to come here and I want to see it in a 360 degrees. I want to experience that as much as I can.

Interviewer: It's also about being right there?

Respondent: It's about being there and what's fun too for me and what will be fun is when I get back to America and the next time I watch a vampire movie or the next time I read the novel I'll be able to say, 'I was there'. And for me, you know, I brought the Dracula novel so the next time that I pick it up and I read it, I will be able to say that this book was in Transylvania. And it's fun too for me because Transylvania is on the other side of the world. So it's so neat to be in such a far away land and you know, when I go home and when I go to bed in Chicago and I'll be able to say, 'I can't believe that I was so far away and I was in this magical, mystical place that I envisioned in my head'. I wonder what in my head it would look like for years and years and you know, this place that has been recreated so many times in movies and this place created in my own mind from the novel. I was actually there and I saw the real thing and I walked, you know, along the pathways. And that to me is … You know, that will be just a treasured memory because I did it as much as I could. I didn't just think about it, I didn't just, you know, romanticize in my head what it would be like. I didn't just try to visualize what it was. I went out and I spent the money and I did the legwork and I am actually seeing it and experiencing it on my own.

Interviewer: It's also a bit of a convergence between imagination and …

Respondent: And reality?

Interviewer: Yeah, reality. Because the tours are about the fictional character, but also about the historical narratives. How do these historical narratives fit in?

Respondent: Ummm …

Interviewer: Have you experienced like a de-mystifying aspect or did you consider it to be an interesting contribution?

Respondent: Well it's interesting because again just from my understanding of Dracula, the reason why Dracula is named Dracula is because Bram Stoker came upon this guy Vlad Tepes, Vlad the Impaler. So it really is his imagination that basically just completely and forever intertwined, because he just obviously took his last name for the character for the vampire. So for me it's equally as interesting, because I get to learn about … I mean not only kind of experience my little, you know, fantasy about being a character in the book Dracula, but also learning more about the actual man who Dracula was, the vampire was based on. To give some historical, you know, weight to the character. But it's in the more and I think anyone who reads the novel and gets interested will go back and go, 'Oh! Vlad Tepes, who is this?', and so I've done that. But the more I study him the more interesting he is to me and the more interesting his life is. Granted there is the … I guess gory aspect of his life and his, you know, the way he tortured people and whatnot. Which is kind of like the car accidents, you can't look away. You're fascinated by something so disgusting.

Interviewer: Do you see these worlds as two different worlds? The historical and the fictional? Or is the one complimentary to the other?

Respondent: You know, one does add to the other, but it is interesting because this is really a two-tiered trip for me. It's learning about the actual history, but then there's also the fantasy, the mystic side of being a character in the novel. But, in the end I guess they are kind of married, aren't they, because they are … Because Bram Stoker just intertwined it so well and used, you know, aspects and to kind of just … Of course he tweaked it just a little bit and threw the vampire legend on this person. But when you think of Vlad the Impaler, you know Vlad Tepes, you think of impaling and blood and of course things vampires and blood. It's all married together. So for this trip for me I think it's all married together, learning about Prince Vlad the man and looking at sites that were described so aptly by Bram Stoker and the novel Dracula. It's all intertwined.

Interviewer: But, at the same time like two different rivers or so do you say.

Respondent: Yes. Exactly, it's two.

Interviewer: One of my last questions is: How did you prepare your visit, other than the normal stuff.

Respondent: Yeah. To prepare for the tour … Well apart from the boring packing aspect, I did psyche myself out, like probably everyone else here. I watched a slew of Dracula movies to get myself in the mindset.

Interviewer: You watched them all or a couple of them?

Respondent: Well I tried to watch, you know, the basic. You have your Max Schreck, Nosferatu from 22, you have your 31 Bela Lugosi, you have your 1958 Christopher Lee Dracula. Yeah, I hit those.

Interviewer: All the classic horror Dracula movies, great. Talking about this horror aspect or the gothic aspect, how does that influence the experience of being here? For instance, you could also go on like the Sound Of Music Tours through Salzburg, but that would be quite different I guess?

Respondent: [laughing] Yes. Well it would and I think that probably goes back to what kind of a person you are and your interests. And for me I have been probably more interested in the macabre and so I think that kind of adds to it. You know, the macabre aspect. Because, yeah you do the sound of music tour that's all nice and fluffy, but I always loved the dangerous aspect. I'd always love horror movies because you know I love that element of dangerous and survival techniques. And I think too … you know it took me a long time to pinpoint this, it only hit me in the late twenties … Why I like horror movies so much is because it gives me a sense of security. Because like I said I get so emotionally invested in the movies and books whatnot and it's kind of fun because after the movie is over it's like I feel much more secure. Because I came of my couch and now I am safe in my bed.

And for a while I really feel like I am in this dangerous situation and you know that sense of security is …

Interviewer: It's also a safe way of experiencing danger.

Respondent: Exactly. That's a great way to put it. It's a safe way of experiencing danger. And that too was, you know, part of it. Like the bad guys. It's a safe way to experience something dangerous, you know? I think that bad guys are more interesting anyways. You know, when you think about Star Wars, there are the heroes, but Darth Vader was … you know, he was always the most interesting character. Well because I think most people don't act out on their bad tendencies. So I guess when you come across a person who does that, you go, 'Well why does he?' And what turned that switch? And of course for Vlad he's human. What made him go to some of his extremes to keep his country inline and his punishments? And you know in warfare him being so brutal and obviously it is brutal anyways, but him kind of taking it up a notch, you know, you are interested. Like well how did he come to that and did he know what he was doing and so that's a very interesting character study. And you know, fictionally, again with Dracula going back it's interesting. One could argue he enjoys being mortal or immortal I should say! Does he enjoy, you know, everything that comes with immortality? Or does he really want to die? Some people have made the arguments and there have been movies that have tapped into that that maybe he does want to die, maybe he does hate himself and hates his existence. You know …

Interviewer: He wants to get caught?

Respondent: Yeah. Exactly! I am trying to think of the word, but I can't think of the word. But, that's interesting to me. For me it's always been about horror movies and I like that just enough of a fantasy aspect too. And that to me is much more that sense of danger, like you said that sense of safe danger. You know?

Interviewer: And doing this trip is the same? A safe way of going into a dangerous landscape.

Respondent: Exactly. You know like I said I will be able to forever kind of … you know? When I go back that first night and I sleep in my bed I will be able to curl up and be safe in my bed. I will be able to say that I was there in the wilds of Transylvania. Boy if this Dracula was a real guy and I was going in Jonathan Harker's footsteps, you know, here I am safe and happy ending. You know, I get the girl. There's that aspect that I enjoy.

Interviewer: Your Mina is waiting at home.

Respondent: That's it.

Interviewer: OK, these were all my questions. Was there anything else that you would like to discuss?

Respondent: Uhm … No.

Interviewer: Well thanks a lot then.

Respondent: Thank you very much.

Filmography

Baantjer (TV series, 1995–2006). Endemol Productions, Netherlands.
Battlestar Gallactica (TV series, 1978–1979). Universal TV, USA.
Bladerunner (1982). The Ladd Company, USA, Japan.
Bram Stoker's Dracula (1992). American Zoetrope, USA.
Braveheart (1995). Icon Entertainment International, USA.
Coronation Street (TV series, 1960–2010). Granada Television, UK.
Dracula (1931). Universal Pictures, USA.
Dracula: Prince of Darkness (1966). Hammer Film Productions, UK.
Dracula: The Un-Dead (2010). Producer unknown (in production).
Harry Potter (movie sequel, 2001–2009). Warner Bros., USA/UK.
Heartbeat (TV series, 1992–2009). Yorkshire Television, UK.
Inspector Morse (TV series, 1987–2000). Zenith Entertainment, UK.
James Bond (movie sequel, 1962–). EON Productions, USA/UK.
Nosferatu, eine Symphonie des Grauens (1922). Prana-Film GmbH, Germany.
Seachange (TV series, 1998–2000) Artist Services. Australia.
Sex and the City (TV series, 1998–2008). Home Box Office, USA.
Smallville (TV series, 2001–2011). Warner Bros., USA.
The Beach (2000). Figment Films, USA/UK.
The Da Vinci Code (2006). Colombia Pictures, USA.
The Inspector Morse (TV series, 1987–2000). ITV Productions, UK.
The Lord of the Rings (movie sequel, 2002-2006). Warner Bros., USA.
The Sopranos (TV series, 1999–2007). Home Box Office, USA.
Wallander (TV series, 2005–2010). Yellow Bird Films, Germany/Sweden.
X-Files (TV series, 1993–2002). 20th Century Fox Television, USA/Canada.

References

Adams, G. (2007). Morse: The No.1 Gentleman Detective. *The Independent*, 27 April 2007.

Aitken, S.C. and Dixon, D.P. (2006). Imagining Geographies of Film. *Erdkunde: Archiv für wissenschaftliche Geographie* 60(4): 326–36.

Andras, C.M. (1999). The Image of Transylvania in English Literature. *Journal of Dracula Studies*, 1. Available at: http://www.blooferland.com/drc/index.php?title=Journal_of_Dracula_Studies [accessed: 1 October 2008].

Armando (1998). *Het schuldige landschap*. Amsterdam: Voetnoot.

Baron, C. (2003). Doctor No: Bonding Britishness to Racial Sovereignty. In C. Linder (ed.) *The James Bond Phenomenom: A Critical Reader*. Manchester: Manchester University Press, 135–50.

Baudrillard, J. (1981). *Simulacres et simulation*. Paris: Galilée.

Baumer, I. (1977). *Wallfahrt als Handlungsspiel: Ein Beitrag zum Verständnis religiösen Handelns*. Bern: H. Lang.

Beeton, S. (2005). *Film Induced Tourism*. Clevedon: Channel View Publications.

Bennett, T. and Woollacott, J. (1987). *Bond and Beyond: The Political Career of a Popular Hero*. London: MacMillan Education.

Betz, P.M. (2006). *Lesbian Detective Fiction: Woman as Author, Subject and Reader*. Jefferson, NC: McFarland.

Black, J. (2002). *The Reality Effect: Film Culture and the Graphic Imperative*. London: Routledge.

Boer, P. de and Frijhoff, W. (1993). *Lieux de mémoire et identités nationales*. Amsterdam: Amsterdam University Press.

Brooker, W. (2005). The Blade Runner Experience: Pilgrimage and Liminal Space. In W. Brooker (ed.) *The Blade Runner Experience*. London: Wallflower, 11–30.

Brooker, W. (2007). Everywhere and Nowhere: Vancouver, Fan Pilgrimage and the Urban Imaginary. *International Journal of Cultural Studies* 10(4): 423–44.

Brown, J. (1997). Draculafilm: 'High' and 'Low' Until the End of the World. In C.M. Davison (ed.) *Bram Stokers Dracula: Sucking Through the Century, 1897–1997*. Toronto, Oxford: Dundurn Press, 269–82.

Bruno, G. (2003). Collection and Recollection: On Film Itineraries and Museum Walks. In R. Allen and M. Turvey (eds) *Camera Obscura, Camera Lucida: Essays in Honor of Annette Michelson*. Amsterdam: Amsterdam University Press, 231–60.

Bryman, A. (2004). *Social Research Methods*. Oxford: Oxford University Press.

Caughey, J.L. (1984). *Imaginary Social Worlds: A Cultural Approach*. Lincoln, NB: University of Nebraska Press.

Cavell, M. (1993). *The Psychoanalytic Mind: From Freud to Philosophy.* Cambridge, MA: Harvard University Press.

Cavender, G. (1998). In 'The Shadows of Shadows': Television Reality Crime Programming. In M. Fishman and G. Cavender (eds) *Entertaining Crime: Television Reality Programs.* New York, NY: Aldine de Gruyter, 79–94.

Cavender, G. and Bond-Maupin, L. (1993). Fear and Loathing on Reality Television: An Analysis of 'America's Most Wanted' and 'Unsolved Mysteries'. *Sociological Inquiry* 63(3): 305–17.

Chapman, J. (2007). *License to Thrill: A Cultural History of the James Bond Films.* London: Tauris.

Clark, D.B and Doel, M.A. (2005). Engineering Space and Time: Moving Pictures and Motionless Trips. *Journal of Historical Geography* 31: 41–60.

Cohen, J. (1986). Promotion of Overseas Tourism Through Media Fiction. In W.B. Joseph and L. Moutinho (eds) *Tourism Services Marketing: Advances in Theory and Practice.* Cleveland, OH: American Marketing Association and Cleveland State University, 229–37.

Coleridge, S.T. (1817). *Biographia Literaria* [or] *Biographical Sketches of My Literary Life and Opinions.* London: Rest Fenner.

Couldry, N. (2000). *The Place of Media Power: Pilgrims and Witnesses of the Media Age.* London: Routledge.

Couldry, N. (2003). *Media Rituals: A Critical Approach.* London: Routledge.

Couldry, N. (2008). Pilgrimage in Mediaspace: Continuities and Transformations. *Etnofoor* 20: 63–74.

Craig, P.R. (1998). Character and Locale in Crime Fiction. *Writer,* 111, nr. 5, 13–15.

Creswell, T. and Dixon, D. (2002). Introduction: Engaging Film. In T. Creswell and D. Dixon (eds) *Engaging Film: Geographies of Mobility and Identity.* Lanham, MD: Rowman & Littlefield, 1–10.

Crouch, D., Jackson, R. and Thompson, F. (2005). *The Media and the Tourist Imagination: Converging Cultures.* London: Routledge.

Culler, J. (1981). Semiotics of Tourism. *American Journal of Semiotics* 1(1): 127–40.

Davis, H. (2001). Inspector Morse and the Business of Crime. *Television & New Media* 2(2): 133–8.

Deleuze, G. and Guattari, F. (1988). *A Thousand Plateaus: Capitalism and Schizophrenia.* London: Athlone Press.

Doel, M.A. and Clarke, D.B. (2007). Afterimages. *Environment and Planning, Part D: Society and Space* 25: 890–910.

Eco, U. (1966). The Narrative Structure in Fleming. In U. Eco and O. Del Buono (eds) *The Bond Affair.* London: Macdonald, 76–85.

Edensor, T. (2005). Mediating William Wallace: Audio-visual Technologies in Tourism. In D. Crouch, R. Jackson and F. Thompson (eds) *The Media and the Tourist Imagination: Converging Cultures.* London: Routledge, 105–18.

Ellis, B. (1989). Death by Folklore: Ostension, Contemporary Legend, and Murder. *Western Folklore* 48: 201–20.

Ellis, B. (2001). *Aliens, Ghosts, and Cults: Legends We Live.* Jackson, MS: University Press of Mississippi.

Fawcett, C. and Cormack, P. (2001). Guarding Authenticity at Literary Tourism Sites. *Annals of Tourism Research* 28(3): 686–704.

Fleming, I. (1963). How to Write a Thriller. *Books and Bookmen* 5: 14–15.

Francois, E. and Schulze, H. (2001). *Deutsche Erinnerungsorte.* München: Beck.

Gibson, S. (2006). A Seat with a View: Tourism, (Im)mobility and the Cinematic-travel Glance. *Tourist Studies* 6(2): 157–78.

Gramsci, A. (1985). *Antonio Gramsci: Selections from Cultural Writings.* Cambridge, MA: Harvard University Press.

Griffin, G.B. (1980). 'Your Girls That You All Love Are Mine': 'Dracula' and the Victorian Male Sexual Imagination. *International Journal of Women's Studies* 3(5): 454–65.

Hanna, S.P. (2000). Is it Roslyn or is it Cicely? Representations and the Ambiguity of Place. *Urban Geography* 17: 633–49.

Hardyment, C. (2000). *Literary Trails: British Writers in their Landscapes.* London: National Trust.

Harrison, R.P. (2005). *The Dominion of the Dead.* Chicago, IL: The University of Chicago Press.

Harvey, D. (1973). *Social Justice and the City.* London: Arnold.

Huppauf, B. and C. Wolf (2009). The Indispensability of the Imagination. In: B. Huppauf and C. Wolf (eds) *Dynamics and Performativity of Imagination: The Image between the Visible and the Invisible.* New York: Routledge, 1–18

Hausladen, G. (1996). Where the Bodies Lie: Sense of Place and Police Procedurals. *Journal of Cultural Geography* 16: 45–63.

Hausladen, G. (2000). *Places for Dead Bodies.* Austin, TX: University of Texas Press.

Herbert, D. (2001). Literary Places, Tourism and the Heritage Experience. *Annals of Tourism Research* 28: 312–33.

Higson, A. (1996). Space, Place, Spectacle: Landscape and Townscape in the 'Kitchen Sink' Film. In A. Higson (ed.) *Dissolving Views: Key Writings on British Cinema.* London: Cassell, 133–57.

Hills, M. (2002). *Fan Cultures.* London: Routledge.

Hobsbawm, E. and Ranger, T. (eds) (1983). *The Invention of Tradition.* Cambridge: Cambridge University Press.

Iwashita, C. (2006). Media Representations of the UK as a Destination for Japanese Tourists: Popular Culture and Tourism. *Tourist Studies* 6(1): 59–77.

Jenkins, O.H. (2003). Photography and Travel Brochures: The Circle of Representation. *Tourism Geographies* 5(3): 305–28.

Johnston, J. (2006). Rosslyn Invests in Preparation for Expected Da Vinci Hordes. *The Sunday Herald,* 16 May 2006: 18.

Karakurum, D. (2006). *Cracking the Da Vinci Code: An Analysis of The Da Vinci Code Tourist Phenomenon* (scriptie). Breda: NHTV Breda University.

Kirshenblatt-Gimblett, B. (1998). *Destination Culture: Tourism, Museums, and Heritage.* Berkeley, CA: University of California Press.

Knight, S. (1980). *Form and Ideology in Crime Fiction.* Basingstoke: Palgrave Macmillan.

Knight, S. (2004). *Crime Fiction, 1800–2000: Detection, Death, Diversity.* Basingstoke: Palgrave Macmillan.

Lefebvre, H. (1991). *The Production of Space.* Oxford: Blackwell.

Legg, S. (2005). Contesting and Surviving Memory: Space, Nation, and Nostalgia in Les Lieux de Mémoire. *Environment and Planning, Part D: Society and Space* 23: 481–504.

Lennon, J. and Foley, M. (2000). *Dark Tourism.* London: Continuum.

Light, D. (2007). Dracula Tourism in Romania: Cultural Identity and the State. *Annals of Tourism Research* 34(3): 746–65.

Lukinbeal, C. (2004). The Map that Precedes the Territory: An Introduction to Essays in Cinematic Geography. *GeoJournal* 59(4): 247–51.

Lukinbeal, C. (2005). Cinematic Landscapes. *Journal of Cultural Geography* 23: 3–22

Malpas, J.E. (1999). *Place and Experience: A Philosophical Topography.* Cambridge: Cambridge University Press.

Mandel, E. (1984). *Delightful Murder: A Social History of the Crime Story.* London: Pluto.

Markozwitz, J.A. (2004). *The Gay Detective Novel: Lesbian and Gay Main Characters and Themes in Mystery Fiction.* Jefferson, NC: McFarland.

McGrath, P. (1997). Preface: Bram Stoker and his Vampire. In C.M. Davison (ed.) *Bram Stoker's Dracula: Sucking Through the Century, 1897–1997.* Toronto, Oxford: Dundurn Press, 41–8.

McManis, D.R. (1978). Places for Mysteries. *The Geographical Review* 68(3): 319–34.

Mordue, T. (2001). Performing and Directing Resident/Tourist Cultures in *Heartbeat* Country. *Tourist Studies* 1(3): 233–52.

Mukherjee, U.P. (2003). *Crime and Empire: The Colony in Nineteenth-century Fictions of Crime.* Oxford: Oxford University Press.

Munt, S.R. (1994). *Murder by the Book? Feminism and the Crime Novel.* London: Routledge.

Muresan, A. and Smith, K.A. (1998). Dracula's Castle in Transylvania: Conflicting Heritage Marketing Strategies. *International Journal of Heritage Studies* 4(2): 86–102.

Nissen, P. (2000). Percepties van sacraliteit: Over religieuze volkscultuur. In T. Dekker, H. Roodenburg and G. Rooijakkers (eds) *Volkscultuur: Een inleiding in de Nederlandse etnologie.* Nijmegen: SUN, 231–81.

Nora, P. (1984–1992). *Les lieux de mémoire.* Paris: Gallimard.

O'Gorman, E. (1961). *The Invention of America: An Inquiry into the Historical Nature of the New World and the Meaning of its History.* Bloomington, IN: Indiana University Press.

Plate, L. (2006). Walking in Virginia Woolf's Footsteps: Performing Cultural Memory. *European Journal of Cultural Studies* 9(1): 101–20.

Poe, E.A. (1841). The Murders in the Rue Morgue. In *Graham's Magazine* 18: 166–79.

Post, P. (1995). *Ritueel landschap: Over liturgie-buiten: processie, pausbezoek, danken voor de oogst, plotselinge dood.* Heeswijk-Dinther: Uitgeverij Abdij van Berne.

Pyrhönen, H. (1994). *Murder from an Academic Angle: An Introduction to the Study of the Detective Narrative.* Rochester, NY: Camden House.

Reijnders, S. (2009a). Plaatsen van verbeelding: Een etnografie van de TV detective tour. *Tijdschrift voor Mediageschiedenis* 12(1): 132–55.

Reijnders, S. (2009b). Watching the Detectives: Inside the Guilty Landscapes of Inspector Morse, Baantjer and Wallander. *European Journal of Communication* 24(2): 165–81.

Reijnders, S. (2009c). Schuldig landschap: Over de toeristische aantrekkingskracht van Baantjer, Wallander en Inspector Morse. *Tijdschrift voor Communicatiewetenschap* 37(2): 118–33.

Reijnders, S. (2010a). Op zoek naar James Bond: Media-pelgrimages, fans en masculiniteit. *Sociologie* 5(4): 502–20.

Reijnders, S. (2010b). Op zoek naar Dracula: Plaatsen van verbeelding in Transsylvanië en Whitby. *Vrijetijdstudies* 28(2): 7–22.

Reijnders, S. (2010c). On the Trail of 007: Media Pilgrimages into the World of James Bond. *Area* 42: 369–77.

Reitz, C. (2004). *Detecting the Nation: Fictions of Detection and the Imperial Venture.* Columbus, OH: The Ohio State University Press.

Riley, R. and van Doren, C. (1992). Movies as Tourism Promotion: A 'Pull' Factor in a 'Push' Location. *Tourism Management: Research, Policies, Planning* 13(3): 267–74.

Roesch, S. (2009). *The Experiences of Film Location Tourists.* Clevedon: Channel View Publications.

Rojek, C. (1993a). Indexing, Dragging and the Social Construction of Tourist Sights. In C. Rojek and J. Urry (eds) *Touring Cultures: Transformations of Travel and Theory.* London: Routledge, 52–73.

Rojek, C. (1993b). *Ways of Escape: Modern Transformations in Leisure and Travel.* Basingstoke: Macmillan.

Roosendaal, J.C. (2002). Moord achter de duinen. In J.C. Roosendaal, B. Vuijsje and C. Rippen (eds) *Moorden met woorden: Honderd jaar Nederlandstalige misdaadliteratuur.* Den Haag: Biblion, 19–45.

Schama, S. (1995). *Landscape and Memory.* New York, NY: Knopf.

Schmid, D. (1995). Imagining Safe Urban Space: The Contribution of Detective Fiction to Radical Geography. *Antipode: A Radical Journal of Geography* 27(3): 242–69.

Seaton, A.V. (1998). The History of Tourism in Scotland: Approaches, Sources and Issues. In R. MacLellan and R. Smith (eds) *Tourism in Scotland*. London: International Thompson Business Press, 1–41.

Seaton, A.V. (2002). Tourism as Metempsychosis and Metensomatosis: The Personae of Eternal Recurrence. In G. Dann (ed.) *The Tourist as a Metaphor of the Social World*. New York: CAB International, 135–68.

Siegel, J. (1993). *The American Detective: An Illustrated History*. Dallas, TX: Taylor.

Silverman, D. (2002). *Interpreting Qualitative Data: Methods for Analysing Talk, Text and Interaction*. London: Sage.

Smith, M. (2003). *Issues in Cultural Tourism Studies*. London: Routledge.

Sparks, R. (1992). *Television and the Drama of Crime: Moral Tales and the Place of Crime in Public Life*. Buckingham: Open University Press.

Squire, S.J. (1993). Valuing Countryside: Reflections on Beatrix Potter Tourism. *Area* 5(10).

Squire, S.J. (1994). Gender and Tourist Experiences. Assessing Women's Shared Meanings for Beatrix Potter. *Leisure Studies* 13: 195–209.

Stoker, B. (1897). *Dracula*. London: Archibald Constable and Company.

Sydney-Smith, S. (2006). Changing Places: Touring the British Crime Film. *Tourist Studies* 6(1): 79–94.

Symons, J. (1992). *Bloody Murder: From the Detective Story to the Crime Novel – A History*. London: Papermac.

Taylor, P. (2004). *Goddess on the Rise: Pilgrimage and Popular Religion in Vietnam*. Honolulu: University of Hawaii Press.

Thomas, L. (1995). In Love with *Inspector Morse*: Feminist Subculture and Quality Television. *Feminist Review* 51(1): 1–25.

Torchin, L. (2002). Location, Location, Location: The Destination of the Manhattan TV Tour. *Tourist Studies* 2(3): 247–66.

Tuan, Y. (1974). *Topophilia: A Study of Environmental Perception, Attitudes, and Values*. Englewood Cliffs, CA: Prentice-Hall.

Tuan, Y. (1985). The Landscapes of Sherlock Holmes. *Journal of Geography* 84(2): 56–60.

Turner, V.W. and Turner, E.L.B. (1978). *Image and Pilgrimage in Christian Culture: Anthropological Perspectives*. New York, NY: Columbia University Press.

Tzanelli, R. (2004). Constructing the 'Cinematic Tourist'. The 'Sign Industry' of *The Lord of the Rings*. *Tourist Studies* 4(1): 21–42.

Tzanelli, R. (2007). *The Cinematic Tourist: Explorations in Globalization, Culture and Resistance*. London: Routlegde.

Urry, J. (1990). *The Tourist Gaze: Leisure and Travel in Contemporary Societies*. London: Sage.

Urry, J. (2002). *The Tourist Gaze: Leisure and Travel in Contemporary Societies* (2nd edition). London: Sage.

Van Gennep, A. (1909) *Les rites de passage* [translated into English in 1960: *Rites de passage*]. Chicago, IL: University of Chicago Press.

Walker, G. and Wright, L. (1997). Locating *Dracula*: Contextualizing the Geography of Transylvania. In C.M. Davison (ed.) *Bram Stokers Dracula: Sucking Through the Century, 1897–1997*. Toronto, Oxford: Dundurn Press, 49–74.

Watson, N.J. (2006). *The Literary Tourist: Readers and Places in Romantic and Victorean Britain*. Basingstoke: Palgrave Macmillan.

Wesseling, H.L. (ed.) (2005). *Plaatsen van herinnering: Een historisch succesverhaal*. Amsterdam: Bert Bakker.

Wezel, R. van (1998). Doe-het-zelf: Een klus die nooit geklaard is. In R. Oldenziel and C. Bouw (eds) *Schoon genoeg: Huisvrouwen en huishoudtechnologie in Nederland, 1898–1998*. Nijmegen: Sun, 231–52.

Wheeler, T.B. (2003). *Finding Sherlock's London: Travel Guide to Over 200 Sites in London*. London: iUniverse.

Index

For Product Safety Concerns and Information please contact our EU
representative GPSR@taylorandfrancis.com Taylor & Francis Verlag GmbH,
Kaufingerstraße 24, 80331 München, Germany

Printed and bound by CPI Group (UK) Ltd, Croydon, CR0 4YY
01/05/2025
01858436-0002